William M. Ivins, Jr.

ON THE RATIONALIZATION
OF SIGHT

*With an Examination of
Three Renaissance Texts on Perspective*

Viator

DE ARTIFICIALI PERSPECTIVA

*Reproducing Both the First Edition (Toul, 1505)
and the Second Edition (Toul, 1509)*

A DA CAPO PAPERBACK

Library of Congress Cataloging in Publication Data

Ivins, William Mills, 1881-1961.
    On the rationalization of sight.

    (A Da Capo Press paperback)
    Bibliography : p.
    1. Perspective—Early works to 1800. 2. Alberti,
Leone Battista, 1404-1472. Della pittura libri tre.
3. Pelerin, Jean, d. 1524. De Artificiali perspectiva.
4. Durer, Albrecht, 1471-1528. Underweysung der
Messung. I. Pelerin, Jean, d. 1524. De artificiali
perspectiva. 1975. II. Title.
    [NC749.194 1975]   742   74-22066
    ISBN 0-306-80011-X

First Paperback Printing 1975
ISBN : 0-306-80011-X

On the Rationalization of Sight, published originally in 1938 as Metropolitan Museum of Art *Papers,* No. 8, in an edition limited to 500 copies, is reprinted by special arrangement with Miss Barbara Ivins. The author's text is unabridged. However, the excerpt from *De Artificiali Perspectiva* appended to the first edition has been omitted.

The first edition (Toul, 1505) of *De Artificiali Perspectiva* by Viator (Jean Pèlerin) is reproduced without abridgement from a copy in The Pierpont Morgan Library, New York.

The second edition (Toul, 1509) of *De Artificiali Perspectiva* is reproduced without abridgement from a copy in the British Museum.

The publishers are grateful to Mr. Walter Strauss for his suggestions concerning this project and for the additional bibliographical entries.

Published by Da Capo Press, Inc.
A Subsidiary of Plenum Publishing Corporation
227 West 17th Street, New York, New York 10011

CONTENTS

William M. Ivins, Jr.
ON THE RATIONALIZATION OF SIGHT

Viator
DE ARTIFICIALI PERSPECTIVA
Toul, 1505

Viator
DE ARTIFICIALI PERSPECTIVA
Toul, 1509

NOTE

The "pathetic fallacy" of the following essays is this:

One night in the late spring of 1936 the writer innocently thought to kill the short end of a hot evening by drafting an even shorter footnote to a book on renaissance book illustration. Before morning he had spent hours madly drawing lines with a ruler and was entangled in a subject that, occupying much of his subsequent leisure time, has flung him headlong and bewildered into fields and problems the very existence of which was then unknown to him and of which he now knows little more. On trains and boats that subject has provided him with the best of crossword puzzles, and in hours of lonesomeness and worry with the most efficient and cleansing of diversions.

The following essays are but stumbling and tentative drafts of small parts of that proposed footnote. However, should they direct the attention of a few students of art to some of the problems they lead up to, their publication in their present state will have been justified.

ON THE RATIONALIZATION OF SIGHT

FOR SOME TIME past the present writer has been pursued by the notion that the most important thing that happened during the Renaissance was the emergence of the ideas that led to the rationalization of sight. This is a matter so different from the fall of Constantinople, the invention of printing from movable types, the discovery of America, the Reformation or the Counter Reformation, or any of the other traditional great events of that period, that a hasty account of it seems excusable before embarking upon a detailed examination of the mechanics of the perspective schemes of Alberti, Pelerin (known as the Viator), and Dürer, in which the effort towards that rationalization received its first expression in Italy, France, and Germany.

In order to have ideas about the returns given us about nature by our five senses, it is necessary to have some system of symbols by which to represent those returns and some grammar or rule by which those symbols are given logical relationships. Lacking such symbols, or a grammar for their use, the task of thinking becomes too onerous to be carried very far. A symbol that cannot be exactly duplicated, or, what comes to the same thing, a symbol that of necessity undergoes fortuitous changes of meaning in the course of repetition or duplication, is of very limited usefulness. A system of symbols without logical schemes, both for its interrelations and combinations within itself and, if it symbolize external fact, for its two-way, or reciprocal, correspondence with that external fact, is also of very limited usefulness. However interesting or important such symbols or series of symbols may be for personal intuition they obviously have little or no value for rationalization.

Words as symbols have no meanings except such as they get from general convention or specific agreement as coupled with recognitions arising through concrete experience, and thus are incapable of conveying information about unique characteristics to people who are not acquainted with those characteristics at first hand. It is doubtful whether a recognizable portrait has ever been painted from a verbal description. As yet no symbolization except a very poor verbal tautology has ever been worked out for the returns given us by the senses of taste and smell. At most we can say that strawberries taste like strawberries and that roses smell like roses. The symbolization for the returns given us by the sense of hearing is extremely limited and as yet has proved incompetent to deal with sounds that lie outside the conventional restrictions of the notation of words and music. There is no symbolism that has been able to record or deal with such things as the personal timbre or characteristics of a human voice. The phonograph and the sound cinema, which after all are very recent inventions, while providing a method for the duplication of sounds, provide no symbols for them and no grammar or rules for the combination of such symbols.

The ancient Greeks worked out a highly abstract symbolism for certain very elementary and limited space intuitions and provided it with a most remarkable grammar. The two together are known to us as Euclidean geometry, the origin of which in tactile-muscular intuition is shown by its nearly complete preoccupation with metrical problems and its essential dependence upon congruence. The

7

dominance of tactile-muscular intuition in Greek geometry and the failure of that geometry to take account of visual intuition is exemplified by the fact pointed out by L. Cremona that "most of the propositions in Euclid's Elements are metrical, and it is not easy to find among them an example of a purely descriptive theorem."[1] Although the Greeks worked all around the problem of perspective, as is shown, for example, by their interest in conics, their knowledge of the anharmonic ratio, and their discovery of such theorems as that about the inscribed hexagon to which Pappus's name is attached,[2] they seem never to have realized that there was such a thing as a mathematical problem of perspective. The underlying tactile assumptions of Euclidean geometry are excellently exhibited in its basic postulate about parallel lines. If we get our awareness of parallelism through touch, as by running our fingers along a simple molding, there is no question of the sensuous return that parallel lines do not meet. If, however, we get our awareness of parallelism through

sight, as when we look down a long colonnade, there is no doubt about the sensuous return that parallel lines do converge and will meet if they are far enough extended. Although Euclid was well aware of this (see his *Optics*, Theorem VI) and was explicit about the fact that his famous fifth postulate[3] was a postulate, it was not until the seventeenth century that for the first time a mathematician adopted convergence at infinity as the basis of a definition of parallel lines.[4]

At the very beginning of human history men discovered in their ability to make pictures a method for symbolization of their visual awarenesses which differs in important respects from any other symbolic method that is known. As distinguished from purely conventional symbols, pictorial symbols can be used to make precise and accurate statements even while themselves transcending definition.[5] In spite of this, picturemaking long remained a most inefficient sort of symbolization. There were two great reasons for this inefficiency: one, that no picture could be ex-

(1) *Elements of Projective Geometry*, Oxford, third edition, p. 50.)

(2) For these and other similar instances, see Sir Thomas Heath's *A History of Greek Mathematics*, Oxford, 1921, vol. II, pp. 270, 381, 397, 419, 521, etc.

(3) Euclid's fifth postulate is today perhaps best known through Playfair's eighteenth-century equivalent, that only one line may be drawn through a given point parallel to a given line.

(4) If one remembers correctly, it was Ernst Mach who picturesquely pointed out that if men were fastened immovably to rocks like mollusks in the sea they could have no sensory intuition of Euclidean space. F. Enriques, who has discussed the spatial intuitions that come from visual and from tactile-muscular sensations, has said: "F. Klein a le premier remarqué cette différence entre les propriétés descriptives et les propriétés métriques." (*Encyclopédie des sciences mathématiques . . .*, tome III, vol. I, p. 63, and see also Enriques's *Leçons de géométrie projective*, Paris, 1930, p. 3.) The way in which the tactile-muscular habit of thought inhibited the ancient geometers is very remarkably shown by Heath's account (*op. cit.*, vol. II, p. 521) of Peithon and Serenus (fourth century A.D.). This account is so interesting that I quote it

in extenso. "In the propositions (29–33) from this point to the end of the book Serenus deals with what is really an optical problem. It is introduced by a remark about a certain geometer, Peithon by name, who wrote a tract on the subject of parallels. Peithon, not being satisfied with Euclid's treatment of parallels, thought to define parallels by means of an illustration, observing that parallels are such lines as are shown on a wall or a roof by the shadow of a pillar with a light behind it. This definition, it appears, was generally ridiculed; and Serenus seeks to rehabilitate Peithon, who was his friend, by showing that his statement is after all mathematically sound. He therefore proves, with regard to the cylinder, that, if any number of rays from a point outside the cylinder are drawn touching it on both sides, all the rays pass through the sides of a parallelogram (a section of the cylinder parallel to the axis) — Prop. 29 — and if they are produced farther to meet any other plane parallel to that of the parallelogram the points in which they meet the plane will lie on two parallel lines (Prop. 30); he adds that the lines will not *seem* parallel (*vide* Euclid's *Optics*, Prop. 6)."

(5) In thinking about symbols it is necessary to remember that while some symbols are defined by their

actly duplicated, and the other, that there was no rule or grammatical scheme for securing either logical relations within the system of pictorial symbols or a logical two-way, or reciprocal, correspondence between the pictorial representations of the shapes of objects and the locations of those objects in space.[6]

Until the end of the fourteenth century this was the condition of man's ability to symbolize his sensuous awareness of nature. To it may be attributed much of the failure of classical and mediaeval natural science.

At the end of the fourteenth century or the beginning of the fifteenth century someone somewhere in Europe began to make woodcuts. Originally the woodcut was a mere labor-saving device for the quantity production of sacred images. It was the earliest form of the printed picture. By the end of the fifteenth century men were printing pictures from engraved and etched metal plates as well as from wooden blocks. The printing of pictures provided for the first time a technique which made possible the exact duplication of pictorial symbols for visual awarenesses.[7]

The invention of the printed picture was thus not improbably an event unique in the history of European thought. Very shortly after it happened there was another unprecedented event which, coming in similar fashion to a society that was not prepared for it, took a long time before its mechanics were understood or its implications were recognized. This was Leone Battista Alberti's discovery of a simple but logical scheme for pictorial perspective.

Perspective may be regarded as a practical means for securing a rigorous two-way, or reciprocal, metrical relationship between the shapes of objects as definitely located in space and their pictorial representations. Important as this is to picturemaking in the narrowest sense, it is doubtless even more important to general thought, because the premises on which it is based are implicit in every statement made with its aid. Either the exterior relations of objects, such as their forms for visual awareness, change with their shifts in location, or else their interior relations do. If the latter were the case there could be neither homogeneity of space nor uniformity of nature, and science and technology as now conceived would necessarily cease to exist. Thus perspective, because of its logical recognition of internal invariances through all the transformations produced by changes in spatial lo-

references, other references are defined by their symbols. The more closely a highly organized and purely conceptual subject, such as mathematics, defines its symbols, the wider is the range of variation that may be introduced into the physical forms of the symbols without effecting change in their significance. The more closely symbols (e.g. pictures) define unorganized and concrete subjects, such as the materials of visual sense awarenesses, the narrower is the range of variation that may be introduced into the physical forms of the symbols without effecting change in their significance. Thanks to the pictorial symbol's sensuously immediate definition of its reference, it is basic for many of the recognitions of similarity which must be made before practical knowledge or science is possible.

(6) The only pre-Renaissance statement I have found to show that people were ever specifically aware of the difficulties of a pictorial symbolism that was not accurately repeatable is contained in chapters 4, 5, and 10 of Book xxv of Pliny's *Natural History*. Little more interesting or directly to the point can be desired than this account of why some Greek botanists gave up the attempt to illustrate their books.

(7) The history of the graphic techniques is neither more nor less than the history (1) of the extension of the ability exactly to duplicate the symbols of visual awareness and (2) of the extension of the power of those symbols sensuously to define unique personal characteristics that transcend purely formal or conventional notation. The historians of "fine prints," because of their limited technical approach and also because of their preoccupation with primitive rarities and the very occasional artistic masterpieces, have with remarkable unanimity disregarded both the expansion of the social utility of the graphic media and their functional growth and intellectual importance as tools of knowledge and thought.

cation, may be regarded as the application to pictorial purposes of the two basic assumptions underlying all the great scientific generalizations, or laws of nature.[8]

Alberti's perspective scheme of 1435–1436 (see p. 14 below) marked the effectual beginning of the substitution of visual for tactile space awareness, because its novel procedure of central projection and section[9] not only automatically brought parallel lines together in logically determinable vanishing points, but provided a basis for the hitherto missing grammar or rules for securing both logical relations within the system of symbols employed and a reciprocal, or two-way, metrical correspondence between the pictorial representations of objects and the shapes of those objects as located in space.

Ever since Alberti made his statement, men have been busy, some misunderstanding and some developing it. Leonardo da Vinci and others who understood it reduced it to a form, known as the "costruzione legittima," that was practical for artists.[10] Viator published the variant which is now known in the studios as three-point perspective in his *De artificiali perspectiva* of 1505. Dürer, whose *Unterweysung der Messung* was published in 1525, was acquainted with the method of projection and section, but failed to understand it, as apparently did his immediate German successors. Vignola, in the first half of the sixteenth century, taught both the costruzione legittima and the three-point method, but the substance of his teaching was not published until Eg-

natio Danti's *Le due regole della prospettiva pratica* appeared at Rome in 1583. Guidobaldo del Monte in his prolix *Montis perspectivae libri sex* of 1600 summed up the perspective knowledge of the sixteenth century and worked out a number of elaborate variations but seemingly added little to the basic theory. He is said to have been the first to use the phrase vanishing point ("punctum concursus").

Kepler's postulation, in his *Ad vitellionem paralipomena* of 1604, that parallel lines meet at a point at infinity[11] was the independent mathematical recognition of an operational fact implicit in Alberti's construction and indirectly stated by him in his text (see p. 22 below). It has been said that Kepler's postulation marks off modern from classical geometry.

It was not, however, until the 1630's that for the first time a mathematician of genius attacked the specific problem of perspective. This man, Girard Desargues of Lyons, the greatly admired friend of Descartes and Fermat, opened the way to both the perspective and the descriptive geometries. That Alberti preceded Kepler by one hundred and seventy years, and Desargues by two hundred years, throws much light upon the mathematical knowledge and ability of the fifteenth and sixteenth centuries. Among many other things, Desargues discovered the theorem about perspective triangles now known by his name, and, from purely perspective considerations, he postulated in so many words that parallel

(8) Cf. B. A. W. Russell, *An Essay on the Foundations of Geometry*, Cambridge, 1897, *passim*.

(9) The late Greek geometers on rare occasion utilized this procedure, as for example in propositions 28 and 29 of the fourth book of Pappus's *Synagoge* (see Heath, *op. cit.*, vol. II, p. 380), but would seem never to have realized its possibilities or to have developed it.

(10) The text of leaf 42 recto of Leonardo's Manuscript A (see reproduction, p. 23 below) proves conclusively

that Leonardo was fully aware of the strict two-way metrical correspondence between a correctly made perspective drawing of an object in space and the object itself.

(11) See Charles Taylor's article "Geometrical Continuity" in *Encyclopaedia Britannica*, eleventh edition. The essential passage from Kepler's text is reprinted in H. F. Baker's *Principles of Geometry*, Cambridge, 1929, vol. I, p. 178.

lines in a plane meet at a point at infinity.[12] In 1640, the year after Desargues's *Brouillon proiect d'une atteinte,* his pupil, Blaise Pascal, by the use of its methods, worked out the theorem about the hexagon inscribed in a conic. Thus Desargues and Pascal, between them, developed the two basic theorems of the modern geometry of perspective.[13] Those who think of perspective only as a more or less unimportant subject in the curriculum of an art school should find food for thought in the facts that Desargues is reputed to have been the first to design an epicycloidal gearing,[14] and that every engineering and architectural school now requires that its students have a knowledge of descriptive geometry.

Because of the scattered way in which Desargues published his results — his very important *Brouillon proiect d'une atteinte* was lost

from the end of the seventeenth century until the middle of the nineteenth century — and especially, it would seem, because of the fascination of the field of endeavor opened up by Descartes's almost simultaneous publication (1637) of analytical geometry, the discoveries of Desargues and Pascal were in general ignored until after they had been more or less independently worked out by other men in the late eighteenth and early nineteenth centuries.

In 1798-1799 Monge published his *Géométrie descriptive,* in which, as the result of a remarkable analysis of previous practice and the discovery of its generalized theoretical basis, he may be said to have created modern descriptive geometry.[15] In 1822 J. V. Poncelet, one of Monge's old pupils, published his great classical *Traité des propriétés projectives des*

(12) Desargues, writing in 1636, said: "Quand les lignes suiet sont paralelles entr'elles, & que la ligne de l'oeil menée paralelle à icelles, n'est pas paralelle au tableau; les aparences de ces lignes suiet, sont des lignes qui tendent toutes au poinct auquel cette ligne de l'oeil rencontre le tableau, d'autant que chacune de ces lignes suiet est en un mesme plan avec cette ligne de l'oeil, en laquelle tous ces plans s'entre-coupent ainsi qu'en leur commun essieu, & que tous ces plans sont coupez d'un autre mesme plan le tableau." (See A. Bosse, *Manière universelle de Mr Desargues pour pratiquer la perspective,* 1648, p. 333.) If this be compared with Alberti's construction (see p. 22 below) it will be seen to be a verbal statement of what happens in the operation of that construction. In 1639 Desargues, in his *Brouillon proiect d'une atteinte . . .,* said: "Pour donner à entendre l'espece de position d'entre plusieurs droites en laquelle elles sont toutes paralelles entr'elles, il est icy dit que toutes ces droites sont entr'elles d'une mesme ordonnance, dont le but est à distance infinie, en chacune d'une part et d'autre." (See Poudra's *Oeuvres de Desargues,* Paris, 1864, vol. 1, p. 104.) Desargues's 1636 demonstration of his theorem about perspective triangles will be found at p. 340 of the book by Bosse cited above, as well as in Poudra's edition of Desargues's *Oeuvres.*

(13) H. Wiener, in his "Ueber Grundlagen und Aufbau der Geometrie" (*Jahresber. d. deutsch. Math. Verein,* vol. 1, 1892, p. 47) says: "Diese beiden Schliessungssätze [i.e. the theorem of Desargues about perspective triangles and that of Pascal about the particular case in which the

hexagon is inscribed within a conic degraded to two straight intersecting lines] aber genügen, um ohne weitere Stetigkeitsbetrachtungen oder unendliche Processe den Grundsatz der projectiven Geometrie zu beweisen, und damit die ganze lineare projective Geometrie der Ebene zu entwickeln."

(14) See Chasles's *Aperçu historique sur l'origine et le développement des méthodes en géométrie,* Paris, third edition, p. 86.

(15) "Monge en conçut les idées fondamentales vers 1775, il les élabora lentement et les exposa pour la première fois d'une façon systématique à l'École Normale, an III de la République. Mais il ne fut autorisé à publier ses importantes découvertes que l'an VII, à cause de la crainte éprouvée par le Gouvernement que les étrangers n'en tirent profit pour leurs ouvrages de défense militaires." (M. Solovine, at p. x of the Notice biographique prefacing his edition of Monge's *Géométrie descriptive,* Paris, 1922.) The following sentences from the short "Programme" which Monge himself prefixed to his book are not without interest: "Cet art a deux objets principaux. Le premier est de représenter avec exactitude, sur des dessins qui n'ont que deux dimensions, les objets qui en ont trois, et qui sont susceptibles de définition rigoureuse. Sous ce point de vue, c'est une langue nécessaire à l'homme de génie qui conçoit un projet, à ceux qui doivent en diriger l'exécution, et enfin aux artistes qui doivent eux-mêmes en exécuter les différentes parties. Le second objet de la Géométrie descriptive est de déduire de la description exacte des corps tout ce qui suit néces-

figures: Ouvrage utile à ceux qui s'occupent des applications de la géométrie descriptive et d'operations géométriques sur le terrain, in which projective geometry was finally developed into a full-fledged mathematical discipline.[16] In 1847 von Staudt freed perspective geometry of metrical notions.[17] The development at the hands of subsequent workers has been most remarkable, especially as leading up to the study of the foundations of geometry. Methods have been discovered by which Euclidean geometry and the various non-Euclidean geometries have been so related to projective geometry that Cayley felt justified in his enthusiastic statement that "projective geometry is all geometry."[18]

On the immediately practical side it is hardly too much to say that without the development of perspective into descriptive geometry by Monge and into perspective geometry by Poncelet and his successors modern engineering and especially modern machinery could not exist. Many reasons are assigned for the mechanization of life and industry during the nineteenth century, but the mathematical development of perspective was absolutely prerequisite to it. Professor A. N. Whitehead has somewhere remarked that the great invention of the nineteenth century was that of the technique of making inventions. The inventions of Monge and Poncelet were among the most important of the intellectual

tools which made that great invention possible.

It is interesting to notice that, just as the earliest datable European prints were made during the lifetime of Alberti (1404–1472), so Monge (1746–1818) and Poncelet (1788–1867) were contemporaries of Nièpce (1765–1833) and Fox Talbot (1800–1877), to whose ingenuity we owe the first photography, a form of picturemaking that is not only precisely duplicable but one in which geometrical perspective is so inherent that today the camera is used as a surveying and measuring instrument[19] as well as a tool for the making of precisely duplicable pictures of unique characteristics that transcend notation in terms of convention, for instance, in its use in the attributions of connoisseurship. Photographic pictures have entered so deeply into the consciousness of Western Europe and America that now there are few people who are not unhappy with a modern picture that is too obviously out of photographic perspective.

The most marked characteristics of European pictorial representation since the fourteenth century have been on the one hand its steadily increasing naturalism and on the other its purely schematic and logical extensions. It is submitted that both are due in largest part to the development and pervasion of methods which have provided symbols, repeatable in invariant form, for representation

sairement de leurs formes et de leurs positions respectives. . . . On contribuera donc à donner à l'éducation nationale une direction avantageuse, en familiarisant nos jeunes artists avec l'application de la Géométrie descriptive aux constructions graphiques qui sont nécessaires au plus grand nombre des arts, et en faisant usage de cette Géométrie pour la représentation et la détermination des éléments des machines. . . ."

(16) There are few stories more romantically interesting or intellectually suggestive than those of the early lives of Monge and Poncelet. Poncelet, captured by the Russians during Napoleon's retreat from Moscow, and languishing in prison for several years without books or

papers, preserved his sanity during his enforced idleness by making some of the greatest of all mathematical discoveries.

(17) In the preface to his *Geometrie der Lage* of 1847, he said: "Ich habe in dieser Schrift versucht, die Geometrie der Lage zu einer selbständigen Wissenschaft zu machen, welche des Messens nicht bedarf."

(18) Compare the remark made by Jean Nicod, *Foundations of Geometry & Induction,* London, 1930, p. 182: "The order of views thus becomes the only fundamental space of nature."

(19) See, e.g., H. Deneux, *La Métrophotographie . . .,* Paris, 1930.

of visual awarenesses, and a grammar of perspective which made it possible to establish logical relations not only within the system of symbols but between that system and the forms and locations of the objects that it symbolizes.

In the middle sixteenth century Brunfels and Fuchs issued the first botanies provided with printed illustrations adequate to the symbolization of the unique characteristics of the various plants and flowers. In 1543 Vesalius and John of Calcar produced the first fully illustrated anatomy, that is, the first grammar of the human figure which, naming the various bones, muscles, etc., defined them by exact reference to pictures, which, being printed from unchanging wooden blocks, remained invariant throughout the entire edition. Since that time, thanks in important measure to the availability of methods for the exact duplication of logically arranged pictorial symbols for visual awarenesses, scientific description has proceeded at a constantly accelerating rate. Scientific classification, which was practically impossible for many things so long as such methods were not available, has now because of them made enormous strides. Those methods have perhaps reached some of their most popularly acclaimed achievements in classification in the fields of archaeology, artistic connoisseurship, medical diagnosis, and criminal detection, knowledges and practices that have been completely refashioned since the development of photography and its related processes. Today there are few sciences or technologies that are not predicated in one way or another upon this power of invariant pictorial symbolization.

The constant extensions of the fields of use-fulness of the pictorial symbol that is precisely duplicable and of the grammars of its use have had a most astonishing effect not only upon knowledge but upon thought and its basic assumptions or intuitions. Where the dominant Greek and mediaeval idea of "matter" seems to have been based on tactile and muscular intuitions, the modern one to a very great extent is based upon visual habits and intuitions. Relativity, which now in one form or another runs throughout contemporary thought and practice, is in large measure a development of ideas that were evolved through the study and use of projective transformations.

From being an avenue of sensuous awareness for what people, lacking adequate symbols and adequate grammars and techniques for their use, regarded as "secondary qualities," sight has today become the principal avenue of the sensuous awarenesses upon which systematic thought about nature is based. Science and technology have advanced in more than direct ratio to the ability of men to contrive methods by which phenomena which otherwise could be known only through the senses of touch, hearing, taste, and smell, have been brought within the range of visual recognition and measurement and thus become subject to that logical symbolization without which rational thought and analysis are impossible.[20] The discovery of the early forms of these grammars and techniques constitutes that beginning of the rationalization of sight which, it is submitted, was the most important event of the Renaissance.

(20) Nicod, *op. cit.*, p. 172, speaks of "our so-called visual distance which alone is correct enough for science."

THREE RENAISSANCE TEXTS ON PERSPECTIVE

I.

By common agreement the three outstanding renaissance texts on perspective are those of Alberti, Viator, and Dürer. Alberti's book, the *Della pittura libri tre,* written in 1435–1436, is generally acknowledged to be the earliest statement of a logically coherent and pictorially adequate scheme of perspective representation. The construction worked out by Alberti, and used after him by generations of Italian artists, is currently known as the "costruzione legittima." Viator's book, the *De artificiali perspectiva,* published at Toul in 1505 and pirated at Nuremberg in 1509, contains the first statement of the familiar "three point" or "distance" method. Dürer's book, the *Unterweysung der Messung,* first published in 1525, was for several generations the most advanced German authority on the subject.

The simplest form of the perspective problem is how to throw a square into a geometrically logical projection. As this is a problem in geometrical optics, and not in physiological optics or psychology, its solution may be regarded as a convention, but a convention of such great utility and so exceedingly familiar that for practical purposes it has the standing of a "reality." The two different methods of Alberti and Viator produce identical results, as can be proven by elementary geometrical reasoning. In diagrammatic form the two constructions are as shown in figures 1 and 2. BC is the near side of the square to be projected. The vanishing point, A, is anywhere above BC, and as high above it as the observer's eye is above the plane of the square. The projected right and left sides of the square lie along CA and BA. DA is parallel to BC. In Alberti's system a perpendicular is erected through B, cutting DA at E. The distance between the points D and E in Alberti's system, and between the points D and A in Viator's system, is equal to the distance between the near edge of the square and the observer. In Alberti's system the projection of the fourth side of the square is determined by where the line DC cuts the perpendicular BE. In Viator's system it is determined by where the line DC cuts the line BA. It is interesting to note that the point A can be located anywhere along the line DA and does not have to be centered above the points C and B, and that because of this fact the costruzione legittima and the distance construction have an ostensible exact similarity when the lines BA and BE happen to coincide.

II.

The first thing we must do, would we understand Alberti's rather obscure text,[1] is rapidly to run through it in the hope of arriving at some idea of what his tools and contrivances were and what it was in particular that he was

(1) The page references following my quotations of Alberti's text are to the reprint of the original as given in Hubert Janitschek's edition of *Leone Battista Alberti's Kleinere Kunsttheoretische Schriften.* In making my English versions I have made hard use of the Italian-English dictionaries of Florio (London, 1611) and Hoare (Cambridge, 1925) and even more of the model represented in my illustrations. I have also consulted the translations, into German by Janitschek, into French by Popelin, and by Bartoli and by Domenichi into Italian from a Latin version. In so far as they deal with Alberti's perspective the first three of these translations with their diagrams are ingenious misrepresentations of Alberti's thought. The precedent thus set has been followed by many of the later writers on renaissance perspective. Janitschek's great merit is that he made the original Italian text available.

trying to do with them. This is especially necessary because it is obvious that Alberti, in writing his descriptions, was not thinking wholly in terms of the problems of the ordinary maker of pictures.

In the second paragraph of the third of his Three Books, Alberti says that *the task of the painter is to represent with lines and color with pigments the visible surface of any object upon any given panel or wall in such fashion that, at a certain distance and in a certain position from the center of vision, it may appear as*

In his remarks about light, shadows, and reflections, he says that there is much more to be said about those subjects, as was shown by the miraculous pictures ("miracoli della pictura," p. 67) he had made at Rome. Later he says that no picture can resemble nature unless it is seen at a definite distance,[7] and that he will give the proof of this if he ever comes to write up those "demonstrations" which he had made and which astonished his friends as though they were miracles.[8] A little later on, at a crucial point in the description of his op-

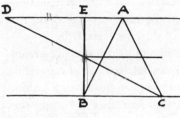

FIG. 1.
ALBERTI'S CONSTRUCTION

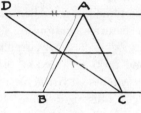

FIG. 2.
VIATOR'S CONSTRUCTION

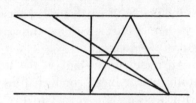

FIG. 3. THE TWO CONSTRUCTIONS
SUPERIMPOSED

though in the round and will closely resemble the object.[2]

In his first book, while describing the lines of vision between the eye and the things it sees, Alberti says: *We may imagine the [visual] rays as though they were very fine threads tightly bound together in a bunch as by an iron band within the eye . . . almost like a pollard of all the rays, the node of which shoots its young branches straight and fine against any opposing surface.*[3] He also says that the rays from the eye to the outward boundaries of the field of vision make what is called the pyramid of vision[4]; that when a painter makes a picture of something he sees it is as if his panel were of transparent glass cutting across the pyramid of vision at a given distance from the eye,[5] and that because of this whoever looks at a picture looks at a cross section of a pyramid of vision.[6]

eration he says that *he determines the distance*

(2) "Dico l'uficio del pictore essere così: descrivere con linea et tigniere con colori, in qual sia datoli tavola o parete simile vedute superficie di qualunque corpo, che quelle ad una certa distanzia et ad una certa positione di centro pajano rilevate et molto simili avere i corpi." — p. 143.

(3) "Et noi qui inmaginiamo i razzi quasi essere fili sottilissimi da uno capo quasi come una mappa molto stretissimi legati dentro all' occhio . . . quasi come troncho di tutti i razzi, quel nodo extenda dritissimi et sottilissimi suoi virgulti per sino alla opposita superficie."—p. 57.

(4) "Et questi razzi extrinsici . . . fanno, quanto si dice, quella piramide visiva." — p. 61.

(5) "Se non che in questa superficie si presentino le forme delle cose vedute, non altrimenti, che se essa fusse di vetro tralucente, tale che la piramide visiva indi trapassasse, posto una certa distantia." — p. 69.

(6) "Chi mira una pictura, vede certa intersegatione d'una piramide." — p. 69.

(7) "Cosa niuna dipinta mai parra pari alle vere, dove non sia certa distantia a vederle." — p. 81.

(8) "Ma di questo diremone sue ragione, se mai scriveremo di quelle dimostrationi quali fatte da noi li amici veggendole et maravigliandosi chiamavano miracoli." — p. 81.

15

he wants between the eye and the picture[9] — a thing that no ordinary painter ever thinks about, or is required to.

The clue to the sense of these remarks is given in the *Vita anonyma* of Alberti (I translate from Janitschek's German, p. 229) which says that Alberti "wrote several books on painting, for with the aid of this art he brought about things unheard of and that the spectators found unbelievable, and he showed these things through a tiny opening that was made in a little closed box. . . . He called these things 'demonstrations,' and they were of such a kind that both artists and laymen questioned whether they saw painted things or natural things themselves."

All these hints point to the strong probability that Alberti conducted his researches with a peep show or a visual model. This being so, before we examine his text critically in detail, let us see what the simplest kind of a peep show or model can be, and find out whether we can use it as a means of arriving at a perspective construction or a diagrammatic rule of thumb for doing easy perspective.

The simplest kind of a model is an oblong box with an eye, or peephole, towards the top of one end, an object on the floor or bottom of the box, and a slide or slides which can be inserted perpendicularly in the box between the hole and the object. On each of the slides such a picture of the object can be painted that when it is in its proper position in the box a person looking through the peephole will find it difficult to tell whether he sees the picture on the slide or the object on the floor. The major problem that faces the maker or operator of such a peep show or model is to determine the shape and size of the picture of the

object to be painted on any given slide, and the position of that picture on the slide. For experimental purposes it is well to use the simplest kind of an object. The best object for an experiment of this kind is a checkerboard, placed on the bottom of the box with its edges parallel to the sides of the box. Once the checkerboard has been placed in position, the next step is to stretch strings from the eyehole to the intersections of the lines on the checkerboard, to represent the lines of vision between the eye and the checkerboard. (See fig. 6, where for clarity's sake strings have been stretched only to the intersections along two adjoining sides of the checkerboard.)

By stretching strings in this way we are enabled not only to make the lines of our vision visible in a fixed position, but after a fashion to leave them there so that we can walk around and examine them from the sides and top and see what we can discover about their angular and measurable relationships to each other, the eyehole, and the object. The size, shape, and height above the floor of the box, of the various cross sections of the pyramid of vision represented by the strings, can easily be measured at any given point between the eyehole and the checkerboard — a proceeding that is fairly difficult without the strings. It is, however, not operationally necessary to stretch strings from all the intersections on the checkerboard, as the same theoretical and practical results can be achieved by stretching them from alternate intersections along any two adjacent sides of the checkerboard and from the remaining corner — which is what we have actually done with our model.

The easiest way of taking our measurements is by resorting to the age-old trick of the carpenters and stonecutters when they have to get the precise shape of a molding or uneven surface, that is, by cutting a templet. A tem-

(9) "Poi constituisco quanto io voglia distantia dall' occhio alla pictura." — p. 83.

plet is merely a piece of thin board one edge of which is gradually and carefully cut away so that when it is finished it will fit exactly up against the molding or uneven surface of which record has to be made. If, then, we cut a templet which will fit over the strings so that it will just touch them as they pass through it and which on either side of the strings will reach down to the bottom of the box, we shall have a way of getting the precise measurements of the cross section of the strings at any point we desire between the eyehole and the checkerboard. The nearer to the checker-

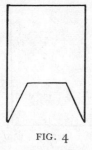

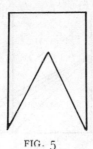

FIG. 4   FIG. 5

board the templet is placed the lower and wider the cross section of the strings will be. The nearer to the eyehole it is placed the higher and the smaller the cross section will be. And, if it is placed right at the eyehole the cross section will be merely a small hole or point at the height of the eyehole from the floor of the box. Thus, if the templet is cut to fit the strings somewhere between the eyehole and the checkerboard it will have a shape more or less like figure 4 and can be slid along the box from its calculated position away from the eyehole but not towards the eyehole, because the strings rise up and get in the way. But if the templet is cut in a triangular form like figure 5, with the top corner high enough to fit over the eyehole and the lower corners far enough apart to fit over the strings where they meet the edges of the checkerboard, the

templet can be slid along the box in either direction and will fit the strings anywhere between the eyehole and the checkerboard. With a templet of this shape the heights of the strings can be marked upon the templet as they are at any given position the templet may occupy. We will use this second form of templet (see fig. 7).

In this way, without knowing anything about geometry or perspective, we have succeeded in discovering a means by which we

FIG. 6

can draw an accurate picture of the checkerboard as seen in perspective on a slide at any position in our box. The trouble with this method is that it will only work for an object small and simple enough to be placed on the floor of the model and to have strings stretched to it from the eyehole of the model. Therefore our next task is to discover some way by which a diagram can be drawn by rule of thumb which will enable us to cope with the problem of the perspective rendering of objects too big or too far away to be put in a model.

One way of doing this is by fixing the templet in a definite position at the near edge of the checkerboard and then looking at our strings from two different positions. The first position from which we look at the strings and templet is from the side. From it we see something like figure 7. We mark the heights of the strings on the templet. We then make a simple schematic diagram to scale of what we have seen (but doing it as though we had seen the model from a point on the line passing through the two points of the templet), like figure 8. We then move around to the end of the model at a position exactly opposite the eyehole, and look at the strings again.

FIG. 7

What we see looks like figure 12. We now make another simple diagram, to the same scale as our first (i.e., fig. 8), of what we have seen, like figure 9, and then by carrying the lines we have marked on the templet across the diagram we have something like figure 10, which is exactly what we have been hoping to find. For if we have the measurements of the checkerboard we want to throw into perspective and know how far away and how much below the eye it is, all we have to do is to make measured diagrams to the same scale from each of our two points of view. One diagram (fig. 8) will give us the apparent heights of the transverse lines on the checkerboard at any given position between our eyes and the checkerboard, and the other diagram will give

us the way in which the orthogonal lines on the checkerboard appear to converge. By carrying our determination of the heights over from our first drawing to our second drawing, we get the picture we want of our checkerboard as seen in perspective. Needless to say, either of these diagrams can be made before the other, and as matter of fact when we come to examine Alberti's text we shall find that he reversed the order in which we have made them.

Before going further, it is well to point out several things about these views and diagrams.

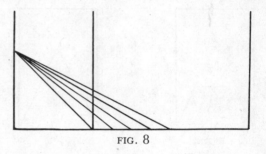

FIG. 8

The most interesting thing about the end elevation of the strings that we made in our second diagram (fig. 9) is that, provided the point of convergence of the strings remains at the same height above the checkerboard and at the same distance from its two orthogonal edges, the diagram remains the same no matter at what angle to right or left the bundle of strings may tilt, as seen in our first diagram (fig. 8). The other thing which it is well to have in mind is that our two views represent the same point of convergence of the strings as seen from different points of view and that the names given to the several representations of that point of convergence in our modern terminology relate not to different things but to different aspects of the one thing as seen from different positions. As most perspective constructions or working diagrams contain indications of the several aspects of the one thing as seen from several points of view it is most convenient to have different names for its different aspects. Alberti called the aspect of the point of convergence shown in the second of our two views the center point, but he used no name for the aspect shown in our first view, which in modern terminology is known as the distance point.

A simpler method, which requires but one drawing and has other very great advantages, could well have been arrived at in the following manner: One day we go to our box to

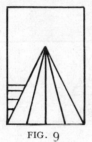 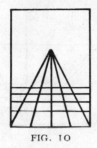

FIG. 9   FIG. 10

make some adjustments in it, and in order to do this we take the triangular templet off the strings, and, temporarily to get it out of our way, we lean it up against the side of the box with its lower angles or points quite accidentally somewhere near the edges of the checkerboard. At the time we do this the templet happens to have marked on it the heights of the strings as they were when the templet was in position directly on the edge of the checkerboard nearest to the eyehole. When we have finished our adjustments and turn to pick up the templet in order to put it back in place over the strings, we notice something we had not seen before which makes us place the templet flat against the side of the box with its lower corners directly in contact with the corners of the checkerboard, so that it looks like figure 11. As soon as we have done

this we see that the perpendicular edge of the templet nearest the eyehole marks the position which the templet had when we marked the height of the strings upon it and that the strings cut across that perpendicular edge exactly at the marks we had made on the templet to indicate the heights of the strings. We then try the templet in various positions over

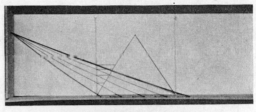

FIG. 11

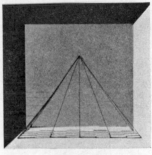

FIG. 12

the strings between the eyehole and the checkerboard, in each case first marking the heights of the strings on the templet, then marking the position of the templet on the side of the box, and finally turning the templet against the side of the box with its edge on the mark we have made on the side of the box. In each case the same relations hold true, and we then make a rather naïve and childish diagram of what we have actually seen in our box, selecting for the purpose the particular case where the templet is flat against the side of the box with its two lower corners touching the corners of the checkerboard. That diagram is like figure 13.

19

We then simplify our diagram a little. First we draw through the point representing the eyehole a line parallel to the line that represents the bottom of the box — because this is the easiest way of getting the points that represent the eyehole and the top corner of the triangular cut in the templet at the same height in our diagram. We then leave out the

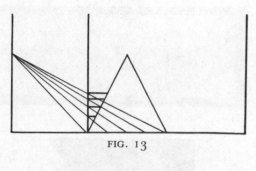

FIG. 13

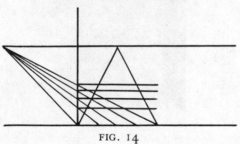

FIG. 14

ends of the box, after which we fill out the broken lines on the templet so that they run across it. These things done, our diagram looks like figure 14. Then, remembering the view from the end of the model (figs. 9, 10, and 12), we indicate the projections of the orthogonal lines on the checkerboard so that our diagram looks like figure 15. We now have a schematic drawing which we can use to throw any checkerboard into perspective. If we know the height of the observer's eye above the checkerboard (i.e. the distance B E), the length of the side of the square (i.e. the distance BC), and the distance of the observer from the square

(i.e. from D to E), we can work out our perspective on paper without having to resort to a box with strings and templet, and by making only one diagram.

After we have done this it does not take long to discover by mere inspection and no theory that a line drawn from one corner of the projected checkerboard diagonally to the far corner will pass through the corners of each of the projected squares it crosses. This diagonal line is represented by a heavy line in the diagram shown in figure 16. After we have looked at this diagram for a little it becomes

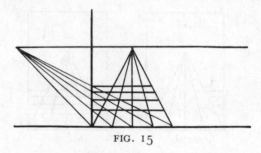

FIG. 15

obvious that all its results can be obtained in an easier manner, as shown in figure 17. From this, by way of the model, its strings, and its checkerboard, to an understanding of how to draw either irregular flat patterns or cubes and other three dimensional objects in perspective is a perfectly simple operational matter.

In many ways the most interesting thing about what we have just done is that we have done it all without any theoretical knowledge of geometry. Starting only with the knowledge that you can't see around a corner (and that therefore any line of vision is a straight line), an empty box, some strings, and a templet, we have worked out a practical method of doing perspective. The most delightful and charming thing about it is that we have done all this without knowing anything about, or even having heard of, such things as vanishing points, or centers of vision, or horizon lines, or central lines, or cones of vision, or ground lines, or picture planes, and especially without any of the intellectual acrobatics involved in mentally revolving imaginary planes with imaginary drawings on them first about imaginary points and then about imaginary axes so that the imaginary drawings on them can come into coincidence with other imaginary drawings on other imaginary planes — all of which even the most elementary books about simple perspective ask us to

nowhere speaks of a vanishing point, a distance point, or a point of vision, an horizon line, or a ground plane or ground line. For this reason in discussing the particular passages in his text that deal specifically with his construction, I shall confine myself to his terminology.

Alberti starts his discussion with a series of theoretical considerations, in which he rationalizes the various things he has found out and invents a number of theoretical planes, lines, and points, which are to be of use to him as names for relations and positions on his per-

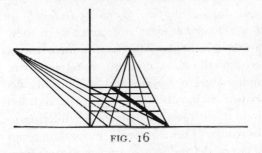

FIG. 16

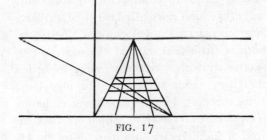

FIG. 17

do, if we want to understand perspective instead of merely following the diagrammatic prescriptions.

The last several drawings that we have made are different forms of the *costruzione legittima*, first described by Leone Battista Alberti in 1435–1436, one of which, as it was drawn by Leonardo da Vinci, is reproduced in figure 18.

III.

Now, having been through all this practical experimenting, let us make our detailed examination of Alberti's text — for unfortunately no pictures that he may have made of the several steps in his operation have come down to us, and so we must do the best we can from his text alone.

Alberti's text is free from all modern terminology and constructional ideas. Thus he

spective construction as distinct from the actual relations and positions in a model. Thus he tells us that the lines of vision, which run from the eye to all points in the field of vision, form a pyramid, or, as we now call it, the cone, of vision, the apex of which is at the eye. He discovers a theoretical line that runs along the axis or center of the pyramid of vision and calls it the central line. When a plane, perpendicular to the central line, cuts across the pyramid of vision it cuts the central line at a point which Alberti calls the center point, and at which all orthogonal lines converge. The only use that Alberti makes of the center point in his construction is one for which we have used the eyehole in our model.

After finishing his theoretical introduction Alberti plunges into a description of how he makes the perspective picture on the slide of

21

his model — though to the discomfiture of his readers he says merely that he will show how he makes a picture ("Principio dove io debbo dissigniere," p. 79) and leaves them to find out about the model and the slides for themselves. The object that he uses in his model and construction is a tessellated pavement, which from an operational point of view is the same as the checkerboard we have used in our model. For this reason in discussing his text I shall treat his word "pavimenti" as though it meant literally checkerboard.

Omitting his unnecessary remarks, for in the fashion of his time Alberti added lengthy classical and other allusions to the many asides that men normally lard their explanations with, let us now examine Alberti's account of his actual method of making a perspective drawing. Without saying so he has taken his position at the end of his model, opposite the eyehole, and, looking at it, he describes the exact way in which we have arrived at the diagram shown in figure 10. He says, *I draw a rectangle,* (which is to bound the picture he is going to draw on the slide of the peep show) *as big as I like, which for me is like an open window through which I see whatever is to be painted,*[10] that is, the checkerboard as seen in perspective. Then, explaining that the bottom of his rectangle and the nearest transverse distance in the field to be represented in his picture are proportional, he marks off the bottom line of his rectangle in as many equal portions as there are squares

along the side of his checkerboard.[11]

Then, by sight, I place within this rectangle a point at the place where the central line of vision comes — because of which it is called the center point.[12] When Alberti says that he places his center point by sight, he is not speaking quite by the book, for his center point is only the name by which he designates the indication on his drawing of the aspect of his eyehole as seen from the opposite end of his box. *Then having located the center point as said, I draw straight lines from that point to all the measured points on the bottom of the rectangle. These lines show me how transverse distances appear to change in length as they get further away to infinity.*[13] In these last three sentences Alberti, without warning, has lapsed into a mixture of references to undescribed operation and to partially described rationalization or theory, and has done it with results that are bewildering to his reader. These sentences, to speak in terms of our model and its operation as distinct from those of Alberti's rationalization, call for a view of the eyehole and the strings as seen from the end of the box opposite the eyehole. This is the view represented in our photograph, figure 12, and diagram, figure 9, except for the marks on the templet.

In this connection it is interesting to notice that Dürer depicts a literal eye at the point at which the orthogonal lines converge in his construction, and in his text calls that point his "nahet aug" to distinguish it from his

(10) "Scrivo uno quadrangolo di retti angoli quanto grande io voglio, el quale reputo essere una fenestra aperta per donde io miri quello que quivi sara dipinto." — p. 79.

(11) "Et emmi questa linea medesima proportionale a quella ultima quantita, quale prima mi si traverso inanzi." — p. 79. Alberti's Latin version states this as follows: "Ac mihi quidem haec ipsa jacens quadranguli linea est proximiori transversae et aequedistanti in pavimento visae quantitati proportionalis." — p. 231.

(12) "Poi, dentro a questo quadrangolo, dove a me paja, fermo uno punto, il quale occupi quello luogo, dove il razzo centrico ferisce; et per questo il chiamo punto centrico." — p. 79.

(13) "Adunque posto il punto centrico come dissi, segnio diritte linee da esso a ciascuna divisione, posta nella linea del quadrangolo, che giace. Quali segnate linee a me dimostrino in che modo, quasi persino in infinito, ciascuna traversa quantita segua alterandosi." — p. 79.

22

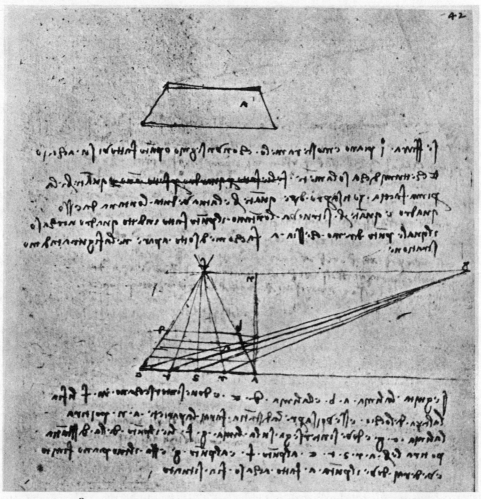

FIG. 18. THE COSTRUZIONE LEGITTIMA AS IT WAS DRAWN BY LEONARDO

TRANSLATION BY C. Ravaisson-Mollien in *Les Manuscrits de Léonard de Vinci, Le Manuscrit A de la Bibliothèque de l'Institut*, Paris, 1881, folio 42 recto: "— Si tu fais un plan [carré] et que tu me le montres avec une marque ou un point qui y ait été fait au hasard, et que tu me dises seulement *s'il est fait en carré parfait ou non, par* combien de brasses a le premier côté, je saurai te dire de combien de brasses ta vue est éloignée de ce carré et à combien de brasses de distance se trouve le point fait au hasard dans ce carré, point que nous supposerons être a; tu devras faire comme il apparaît dans la démonstration ci-dessus figurée.

"— Suis la ligne a b et la ligne d e jusqu'où elles se coupent en f; là se trouve la hauteur de l'oeil. Et si tu veux connaître la distance, tu feras la paroi [l'écran] a n, puis tu traceras la ligne c g; à son intersection avec la ligne g f est le point de distance; tire ensuite les brasses a r s t e au point f et au point g; limite ton plan, et tu verras où le point a, fait au hasard, est situé."

"ander aug," from which he determines the heights of his transverse lines (see p. 35 below). Leonardo, in the drawing to be seen on leaf 36 verso of his Manuscript A likewise indicates a literal eye at each of the two points. There is little doubt that in so far as Dürer understood the Italian tradition, as represented, for example, by Leonardo, he followed it in his construction, and that that tradition goes back to the operational fact that in a model the strings representing the orthogonal lines converge at the eyehole. In any event the drawing that Alberti has just described fits the facts as to both his actual

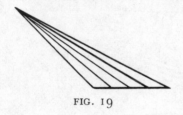

FIG. 19

eyehole and that aspect of it on his drawing which he calls his center point. On it he has indicated the way in which the orthogonal lines on his checkerboard converge as seen in perspective, the outermost of those lines providing a series of limits beyond which the transverse lines on his checkerboard as seen in perspective do not extend.

Alberti now turns aside from his explanation of his own practice to criticize an unscientific method followed by some other people, who try by an arithmetical rule of thumb to indicate the way in which a series of equidistant transverse parallel lines, lying on a plane different from that of the eye, appear to get closer and closer together as they recede from the observer.

Having finished this criticism, he returns to his own problem, saying: *But the way the transverse lines succeed one another is as fol-*

24

lows. Then, but without saying so, he leaves the end of his model, at which he has hitherto been stationed, and moves around to its side, and, looking at it from this different point of view, tells how he represents what he sees. *I take a little space* ("uno picciolo spatio" — doubtless a piece of paper or board on which he is going to work out the measurements that he is going to carry over onto the drawing he has started to make on his slide) *on which I draw a horizontal line, which I divide in as many equal parts as there are in the bottom line of my rectangle. Then I place a point as high above this line as the center point is above the bottom of my rectangle: and from that point I draw lines to each division in this line.*[14] At this stage of his second drawing it looks like figure 19. *Then I determine the distance I want between the eye* (i.e. the point he has just placed, which represents the eyehole in his model, the precise location and height of which he knew because it was fixed in his box) *and the picture* (which is to be painted on the slide he is going to place between the eyehole and the checkerboard in his peep show), *and there I draw what the mathematicians call a perpendicular line across the other lines.*[15] At this stage his second drawing looks like figure 8. He then gives a definition of a perpendicular line, and goes on: *Where this perpendicular line is cut by*

(14) "Ma nella quantita transverse come l'una seguiti l'altra cosi seguito. Prendo uno picciolo spatio nel quale scrivo una diritta linea, et questa divido in simile parte, in quale divisi la linea che giace nel quadrangolo. Poi pongo di sopra uno punto alto da questa linea, quanto nel quadrangolo posi el punto centrico alto dalla linea che giace nel quadrangolo; et da questo punto tiro linee a ciascuna divisione segniata in quella prima linea." — p. 83.

(15) "Poi constituisco quanto io voglia distantia dall' occhio alla pictura, et ivi segnio, quanto dicono i mathematici, una perpendiculare linea tagliando qualunque truovi linea." — p. 83.

the other lines gives me the order of the recession of the transverse lines. And in this way I determine the measurements of all the parallel lines and the squares upon the checkerboard as it appears in the picture on my slide.[16] That is to say, the points where the bundle of converging lines cross his perpendicular give him the heights at which the transverse lines are to be drawn in the picture on the slide, and he is now able to carry them over from his working drawing to that picture and thus complete it so that it looks like figure 15.

Whether these [transverse lines] have been correctly drawn by me [in the picture on my slide] will be shown if a single straight line will form a diagonal through a number of the squares in the picture.[17] His completed picture on the slide, with the diagonal marked upon it, looks like figure 20. It has been said that Alberti used this fact about the diagonal as a proof of the correctness of his drawing, and that in so doing he was mistaken because it is inherent in the geometry of his construction. This criticism, however, is not quite correct, for the critic failed to notice that Alberti had made two drawings and not one; had carried his first drawing as far as he could without certain measurements, and then to get those measurements had made his second drawing; after which, having those measurements, he had completed his first drawing. In consequence of all this he needed some way of checking up the accurate correspondence of the two drawings and sets of measurements.

(16) "Questa cosi perpendiculare linea, dove dall' altre sara tagliata, cosi mi darà la successione di tutti le traverse quantità. Et a questo modo mi truovo descripto tutti e paralleli, cioè le braccia quadrate del pavimento nella dipintura. . . ."—p. 83.

(17) "Quali quanto sieno dirittamente descripti ad me ne sara inditio se una medesima ritta linea continovera diametro di più quadrangoli descripti alla pictura." —p. 83.

The diagonal provided the needed verification in the simplest possible way.

Just when or by whom it was discovered that the construction could be made with one drawing instead of two, by schematically turning the end elevation of the lines of vision into the same plane with the side elevation — that is, what we actually did when we turned the marked templet in our model against the side of the box — is not known. Alberti's text is not sufficiently developed for us to be certain that he knew it although there is every probability that he did. In any event that knowl-

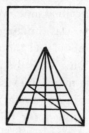

FIG. 20

edge must have followed very shortly afterwards, because Leonardo da Vinci knew all about it, including its strict relationship to actual measurement, as can be seen by examination of Ravaisson-Mollien's facsimile and translation of leaf 42 recto of Leonardo's Manuscript A (fig. 18).

Alberti has now arrived at the end of his technical description of his perspective construction, but he goes on to say: *This being done, I draw a straight line across the picture on my slide from side to side, parallel to its bottom line and passing through the center point, and thus divide my picture. This line serves as a limit above which nothing in the picture can extend that is not higher than the eye of the observer. And because this line passes through the center point I call it the central line. From this it follows that the fig-*

25

ures painted on the furthest squares of the picture are smaller than the others; as Nature demonstrates to us.[18] This statement is interesting as showing how near Alberti came to discovering the idea of the horizon line, which in effect he had when he had drawn his line across his diagram through its center point.

It is worth while to go back, at this place, and consider a little more fully Alberti's phrase about determining the distance between the eye and the picture (see p. 15 above) — for it is this phrase which, although one of the greatest stumbling blocks to an understanding of his text, contains the key to the operation described in it. When he wrote his description he was thinking in large part in terms of his model and the things that he actually did with it. Thus the position of the slide (which for many purposes is identical with the templet in our model) was the only variable he mentioned, for the eyehole and the checkerboard were built into his box so that in his experiments their locations and measurements were constant — though no one knew better than he did that if the eyehole were made higher or lower or moved to one side or the other, or if the checkerboard were slid along the bottom of his box in either direction, then the size and height of the checkerboard as represented on his slide (or, in terms of our model, the pattern of the points where the strings pass through the templet) would be different, and the lines of vision (or

strings) would make different angles with each other both at the eyehole and at the floor of the box. Every man who actually works with a tool or device such as the model I have described knows this kind of thing simply from working with it, and needs no explanation of it, verbal or otherwise. The principal reason for his usual failure to call attention to it or to explain it is its complete operational obviousness to him.

One of the greatest difficulties that men have in understanding explanations arises from the fact that the explainer tacitly thinks in terms of one particular tool or operation with its inherent, disguised factors, and the explainee tacitly thinks in terms of a different tool or operation with its different inherent, disguised factors. It was this even more than Alberti's obscurity of expression that for a long time prevented his discovery from becoming known among the artists. Where Alberti thought in terms of a picture on a movable slide in a model, the ordinary artist was trying to learn how to make a picture that could hang or be painted on the wall of a room and that would appear to be adequately in perspective no matter what its distance was from the eye of its beholder. This difference in problem can be phrased by saying that as between the constants and variables of Alberti and the ordinary painter, the only thing in common was the constancy of the size of the checkerboard. Because of this it took the painters in general a long time to discover that Alberti's construction could be adapted to their purpose by simply anchoring the picture plane to the checkerboard in such a way that the bottom line of their picture coincided with the near transverse edge of the checkerboard, and that once this was done the only measurements they required were those representing (1) the dimensions of the checker-

(18) "Fatto questo, io descrivo nel quadrangolo della pictura ad traverso una dritta linea dalle inferiore equedistante, quale dal uno lato all' altro passando su pel centrico punto divida il quadrangolo. Questa linea a me tiene uno termine, quale niuna veduta quantità non più alta che l'occhio che vede, più sopra giudicare. Et questa perchè passa pel punto centrico dicesi linea centrica. Di qui interviene che li huomini dipinti, posti nell ultimo braccio quadro della pintura sono minori che gli altri; qual cosa cosi essere la natura medesima ad noi dimostra." — p. 83.

26

board, (2) the distance between the observer and the near side of the checkerboard, and (3) the height of his eye above it, that is, three measurements which were so fixed and obvious in Alberti's particular operation that he forgot even to mention two of them. This anchored position of the picture plane is that actually illustrated in the photographs of our model.

IV.

On turning from Alberti to Viator, we find another construction, which, as pointed out above, has precisely the same results as that of Alberti. Thanks to The Pierpont Morgan Library it is possible to give in an appendix a facsimile of Viator's French text, which seems not to have been reprinted in modern times. Because of the light that they throw upon Dürer Viator's schematic diagrams are here reproduced from the Nuremberg piracy.

As Viator acknowledges in his last paragraph, his diagrams are of much greater importance than his text, and for their understanding require not so much words as a sense for the business in hand. His text, however, is interesting, because it contains in all probability the first printed references to the ground plane, the horizon line, and the "tiers points" from which his system got its name of three-point perspective. The most important single statements in his text are those in which he says that his center point and his two distance points are located on a line at the level of the eye, and that his two distance points are "equedistans du suiect: plus prochains en presente, et plus esloignez en distant veue." As otherwise his words add very little to the analysis we have to make, we shall, to save time, confine ourselves to his diagrams.

Just as Alberti, in his text, starts off with a series of rationalizations of his actual operation and then proceeds to describe his opera-

tions in terms of his rationalizations, so Viator follows the same procedure in his drawings. He begins with two theoretical explanatory constructions and ends with the three simplified diagrams of his actual working construction — thereby, like the writers both of detective stories and of studies like this, reversing his actual order of work and telling the story of his discoveries backwards.

The typical working diagram for Viator's construction is his third woodcut (fig. 26). We are familiar with this, as still further simplified, in figure 21 (see also p. 15). It has been

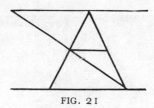

FIG. 21

suggested that this diagram, or construction, possibly represents a tradition or method that had been in use among the French masons of the late Middle Ages and early Renaissance, but, so far as I have been able to discover, no specific reasons for this conjecture have been adduced. It may well be based simply upon Viator's textual use of several terms that formed part of the French masons' vocabulary — a species of argument that if applied to the present study would result in the charming discovery that it represents a tradition among American carpenters.

Often as it has been pointed out that Alberti's and Viator's constructions give identical final results, it seems to have been considered that in its simplified form (as in fig. 21) Viator's construction is much more abstract than Alberti's, and that therefore it represents a much more considerable effort of geometrical imagination and knowledge than Alberti's does. I have nowhere met any sug-

27

gestion as to how it might have had its origin in an operation, as distinct from the geometer's theorems and analysis. It would seem, however, that it may well have evolved from a simple mechanical operation. If we again revert to the use of a model, this will be apparent — as will also be the fact, which seems not to have been mentioned hitherto, that in spite of its apparent unlikeness to the construction of Alberti the construction of Viator represents the same series of operations with but one very slight modification.

If we may predicate that Viator, a much

FIG. 22

traveled and intelligent man, hearing or learning that Alberti, as the *Vita anonyma* says (see p. 16 above), "showed these things through a tiny opening that was made in a little closed box," himself began to experiment, much as we have done, there will be no difficulty in working out a way by which he might have discovered his particular construction. As we have seen, Alberti, by working with a model such as that which we have used, could well have discovered the costruzione legittima by merely swinging his templet against the side of his box in such a position that its two lower corners came in contact with the corners of the checkerboard. In doing this the templet was swung as though it were a door hinged to the side of the box in such a way that its two lower points could coincide either with the two corners of the checkerboard nearest the eyehole or with the

two corners of the checkerboard next to one side of the box.

Viator, using a similar apparatus, could have achieved his particular construction by revolving his templet on its apex as a pivot rather than by swinging it around on its perpendicular edge as a hinge. As revolved in this manner, and not swung, its appearance and relationships are shown in our photograph, figure 22, in which, to make the matter more obvious, several of the unimportant strings have been omitted. Comparison of this photograph with the preceding simplified schematic diagram (fig. 21) shows that this abstract geometrical construction is, like the costruzione legittima of Alberti, very little more than a childishly naïve picture of something that can actually be seen in a simple model.

By revolving his templet about its apex, Viator kept that apex in its original position, directly above the center of the near edge of the checkerboard, while Alberti, by swinging his templet doorwise about a perpendicular edge, moved the apex of the templet away from its original position to one directly above the center of an orthogonal edge of the checkerboard, and thus left only the hinge edge of the templet in its original position perpendicular to the near edge of the checkerboard. This shift in the position of the apex of the templet explains why it is that although the crucial distance between the near edge of the checkerboard and the observer is measured off, in Viator's scheme, from the apex of the templet, or center point, in the costruzione legittima it is measured off from the perpendicular — for each of them, apex and perpendicular, in its particular construction, stands for the near edge of the checkerboard. It was because Dürer did not clearly understand this basic operational difference between the two

FIG. 23. WOODCUT OF VIATOR'S LIVING ROOM

systems that he came to grief in his own perspective scheme.

Whether or not Viator's solution of the problem was worked out first by Viator himself or by some artist, builder, or craftsman, there is, of course, no way of knowing. It is quite possible that Alberti, while working with his model, may have discovered it, and also that he discarded it for his other discovery of the costruzione legittima, because this latter, by enabling him to draw the pictures he needed in the correct sizes and at the correct heights on the several slides of his model, made it possible for him to make his academic "demonstrations" of his theory about the pyramid or cone of vision and its cross sections.

To return to Viator's diagrammatic illustrations: Just as he revolved his templet (instead of swinging it against the side of his box), so in his first diagram (fig. 24), intent on theory or rationalization, he represented at the bottom of a pyramid of vision, the circle which was the trace of the two lower points of his templet as it revolved about its axis (the apex of the pyramid being the apex of his templet and the perpendicular the axis). His second diagram (fig. 25) shows the same pyramid, but with its bottom tilted back as seen in perspective. His third diagram (fig. 26) is a schematic simplification of his second. His remaining diagrams (figs. 27, 28, and 29) are no more than various applications of the construction arrived at in his third diagram. His third diagram, however, was the all-important one — and it is only a slight amplification of our figure 21, which, as we have seen, is little more than a naïve picture of what Viator might have seen when he looked into a model. Thus the order in which Viator undoubtedly worked out his diagrams was not that in which he printed them in his

book, but something much more like this: first our figure 21, next his third, then his second, and last of all his abstract and theoretical first diagram.

To anyone who is familiar with fifteenth-century and early sixteenth-century pictures, and especially with the book illustration of that time, the first sight of a copy of the *De artificiali perspectiva*, in either the original Toul edition of 1505 or the Nuremberg piracy, comes with a sort of a shock. The many pictures of known buildings with which Viator exemplified his perspective method are so clear, so reasonable, so just, that they are wholly out of tune with anything that had been done before them or that was done for a long time afterwards. Such a sudden step across the centuries into a completely modern system of pictorial organization and point of view can hardly have happened on any other occasion. Dürer's Saint Jerome in His Study (B. 60) of 1514 is a portrayal of an interior that is famous for its mastery of perspective, but as compared with Viator's representation of his own living room, published nine years earlier at Toul and five years earlier at Nuremberg, it gives no feeling of space and no visual comfort. Where we can believe Viator's picture with our eyes as a truthful report of something that had an actual existence, our attitude towards Dürer's engraving is that with which we listen to a charming but obviously impossible fairy tale, in which there is no reasonability and no hard fact. Our reproduction of the woodcut of Viator's living room (fig. 23) is made not from the Toul original but from Georg Glockenton's coarse copy that was published at Nuremberg. It is presumably the same as that which appeared in the original edition of the Nuremberg piracy five years before Dürer in that same town gave his Saint Jerome to the world.

FIG. 24. VIATOR'S FIRST DIAGRAM

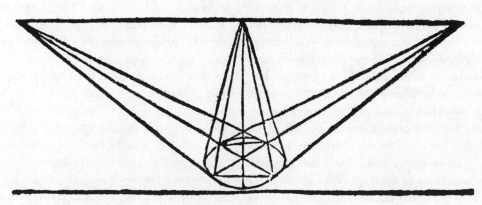

FIG. 25. VIATOR'S SECOND DIAGRAM

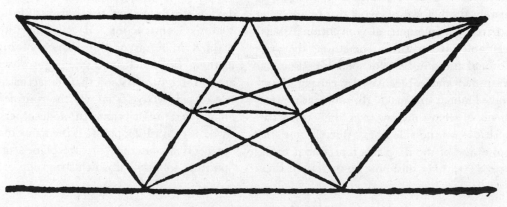

FIG. 26. VIATOR'S THIRD DIAGRAM

V

It has been said that Alberti's great discovery was that the picture plane was a perpendicular cross section of the cone of vision, but there is reason to believe that possibly it was something more and other than that. Until Alberti's time the problem seemingly had been confined to a simple two-term relation between the beholder and the single object, in which the beholder saw only the object and no one saw the beholder. So long as the problem was confined to a particular object as seen through the beholder's eyes it remained strictly insoluble, because the beholder, like John who had hold of the bear's tail, could not stand off and survey the situation. Alberti's great stroke of genius lay in his practical realization that the problem was not to be solved by thinking only about the bear as seen through John's eyes, but that what Henry and Thomas saw from the side lines had to be brought into consideration. In doing this Alberti discarded an insoluble two-term relation and took on a series of relations with enough terms to permit of its solution. In other words Alberti discovered that, pictorially at least, form and position were functions of each other, and thus were relative and not constant, and also that there could be no statement of position in three-dimensional space in anything short of a three- or four-term relation. This again is merely another way of saying that by adopting a particular geometrical convention Alberti was able to substitute something that was rational and objective for something that was irrational and subjective. By getting Henry and Thomas to make diagrammatic statements of what they saw from their respective positions on the side lines, Alberti came into possession of the diagrams reproduced in figures 8 – 15. He told how he correlated these

various statements in that portion of his text analyzed on pages 22 – 25 of this paper. One of the ways in which it may have been discovered that the different statements could all be made in one single diagram has been explained on page 19 of this paper. Later on Viator achieved identical final results by proceeding in a slightly different way, as has been shown on page 28 of this paper.

The solutions of the perspective problem that are associated with the names of Alberti and Viator were based upon the simplest kind of practical ingenuity, and in some respects were little more than clever carpenter's work. The two solutions were full of implicit mathematical relationships, but the men who used them were content with them as easy contrivances that worked. The mathematical analysis of the perspective problem, and of the special variety of geometry that was implicit in Alberti's novel method of projection and section, seems to have been first undertaken, just about two hundred years after Alberti wrote his treatise, by Desargues, who utilized an assumption by which parallel lines concur at a point at infinity (see p. 11 above).

As a result of the work of Desargues and his nineteenth-century followers, there has been developed out of the Albertian perspective construction what is possibly the most generalized discipline of geometrical thought. The ordinary pictorial perspective diagram of to-day, while retaining the outward form of Viator's construction, is customarily explained in terms of this branch of higher mathematics — that is to say, in terms which are so rarely understood that the actual practice of perspective is merely the routine of a memorized prescription. In modern perspective, the "vanishing point" is the name for the "projection" on the "picture plane" of the "point at infinity" at which the group of "or-

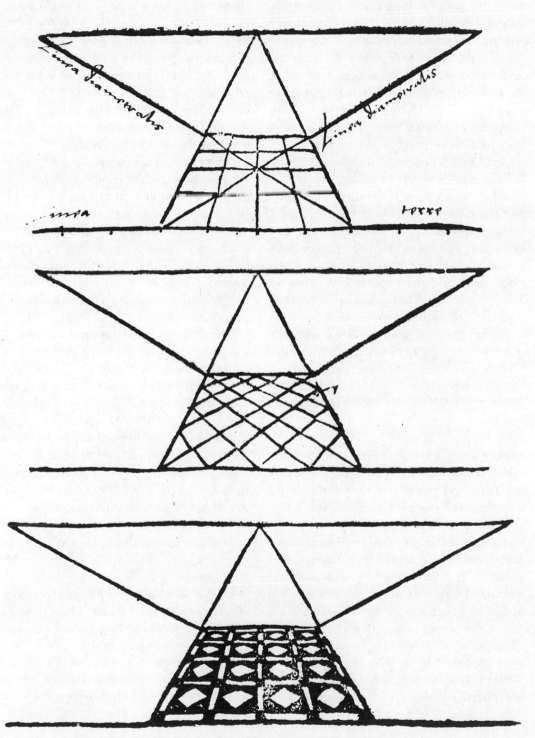

FIGS. 27–29. VIATOR'S FOURTH, FIFTH, AND SIXTH DIAGRAMS

thogonal lines" "converges." The modern vanishing point is thus a matter of highly technical definition. It is not only completely foreign to the renaissance idea of the center point, which, as we have seen, was merely the operational name for a particular aspect of the observer's eye, but it is based upon an assumption completely foreign to the basic assumption of classical geometry that parallel lines could never meet no matter how far extended. Such "questions," therefore, as: "Did the ancients know the vanishing point?" are strictly comparable to such other "questions" as: "Did the ancients know the square root of minus one?" Both the vanishing point and the square root of minus one exist only by virtue of assumptions and definitions first made long after the ancients had ceased to exist. Thus when learned classical scholars translate "obscurum acumen coni" as "the vanishing point of a cone," they not only make nonsense of Lucretius's sensible words but impute to him their own misunderstanding of definitions and technical terms with which he could not possibly have been acquainted.

VI.

Dürer's prominence as an artist, the wide pervasion of his books and prints, and especially the fame and popularity of his theoretical writings, justify us in looking at his actual accomplishment in perspective as closely as possible. Dürer certainly was familiar with the linear appearance of Alberti's diagram, and possibly even with Alberti's account of his method. In spite of what has been accepted as fact by practically all the commentators, I personally cannot believe that Dürer was unacquainted with Viator's diagrams, which were published in the Nuremberg piracy of Viator's book in 1509. That piracy, we must not forget, was the most important book on

the subject of Dürer's predilection printed in Dürer's home town prior to the publication of his own book in 1525. That he should not have seen and known it is utterly incomprehensible except at the cost of his reputation for being really interested in its subject. A set of later impressions of the very rare woodcuts for the Nuremberg piracy is in the Print Room of the Metropolitan Museum, but the text that should accompany them is unfortunately lacking. These woodcuts are coarse but schematically perfect copies of those in the original French edition of 1505. As we have just seen, Viator's woodcuts contain the gist of his matter, and so any possible stupidities in the text that accompanied the pirated copies of them can hardly constitute an excuse for any failure to understand them on the part of a great man with a great reputation as a scientific thinker.

The difficulty that Dürer had with the perspective systems of his two predecessors was doubtless due to his failure to understand the operational bases from which they had been evolved. In all likelihood it was the operational basis of Alberti's system that Dürer wanted so much to learn about during his second Italian trip — and that he never did learn about. When we come to look at the celebrated diagram 59 in Dürer's *Unterweysung der Messung* and his attempted explanation of its construction, we shall see that he came to grief precisely in those places where his predecessors were not explicit about what they were doing.

Where Alberti had a model containing a checkerboard, Dürer had a cube standing on a square surface, and his problem was to represent in perspective the shadow cast by the cube on the square surface. Before he could throw either his cube or its shadow into perspective he felt that he had to throw the square

34

surface itself into perspective. For practical purposes this last problem was identical with the problems of both Alberti and Viator, but it was so differently expressed and was undertaken with such a different purpose that the identity was perhaps not as obvious as it might have been.

Dürer had two methods of arriving at his picture of the cast shadow, one longer and more complicated, the other shorter and easier. This easier one was his celebrated "nahere weg," as he called it, and the one on which his fame as a master of the theory of perspective is based. Dürer's text of this, in so far as it deals with the projection of the square surface on which his cube rested, is given at the bottom of this page.[19] in a facsimile from the 1538 edition of his *Unterweysung der Messung*. His diagram 59 is reproduced as figure 30.

In his description of his nahere weg Dürer starts with a transverse line drawn across his paper. A little above the left end of this and parallel to it he draws another line *g f* of the same length as the edge of the square surface to be projected in perspective. Above the line *g f* he indicates a near point of sight ("ein nahet aug") with an eye, placing it at the same distance above that line that it occupied in one of the diagrams for his more complicated construction (none of which is here reproduced) — which was anywhere that he wanted to put it. From this near point of sight he draws lines to the points *g* and *f*. In this way he has indicated the near side of the square surface as seen in perspective and the directions of the two orthogonal sides. His remaining problem is where and how to draw his fourth side. Off to the right, and at the same height as the near point of sight above his transverse line, he indicates a second point of sight ("ein ander aug") by drawing another eye, but this time placing it in the head of a man who stands with his feet on the transverse line. The distance at which this second point of sight is set off is the same as in Dürer's

(19)

Ernach wil ich durch eyn anderen vnd nehern weg/gleich das vorbeschriben ding abgestolen/in das gemel leren pringen. Durch ein solchen weg.

Leg vber zwerch ein lini in der leng der vorigen.e.f.g.h.des forderen außgezognen grundes/die da an stat einer gefierten ebnen ist/ vnnd setz ein nahet aug auf der seiten ob der lini .f. wie dann das vor auf dem puncķten des augs der kreütz linien stet bey dem vor beschriben ding.

So das gemacht ist als dann zeuch auß disem aug zwo gerad lini an bede ort der nider gelegten lini.e.f.g.h.die machen vnden zwey eck /vnd der sierung sind drey seiten gemacht die viereckēt abgestolen sollen sein . Nün must du die hinder seiten wissen zu machen /wie hoch sie vbersich steygt/ das sind also. Stel ein ander aug auf die seitten in der weyte wie das bey dem vor beschribnen grund stet aber gleych in der höch wie das neher aug.auß disem aug zeuch zwo gerad linien an bede ort der für, gelegten linien. Darnach reyß ein aufrechte lini.aa.bb.die daß forder eck an rürt/wo dann dise auf, recht lini abschneydt/die lang streym lini die auß dem weyterem aug in den spitzigen winckel zogen ist in den puncķten setz.cc.Auß disem puncķten.cc.zeuch ein zwerch par lini durch die zwo streym lini, en die da auß dem nahetten aug auf die zwey vnderen ort der zwerchlini der sierung zogen sind.wo dvnn die streym linien durch schneiden werden/da machen sie zwey eck/also ist dise gefierte/ebne rechte abgestolen/gleych wie die vor gemacht/darumb bezeychen auch ir vier eck mit den vier bustaben.e.f.g .h.wie hie voren im ersten gethan ist. Diß hab ich hienach also aufgerissen/ee ich weyter gee.

35

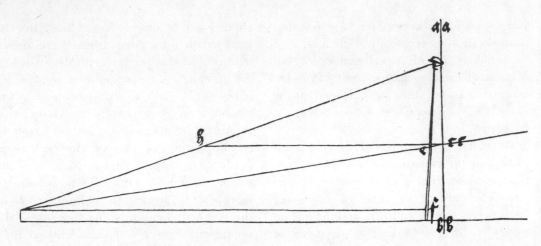

FIG. 30. DÜRER'S

more complicated construction. In his description of his more complicated construction Dürer says that he puts the second point of sight as far from the square surface as he likes ("so weyt . . . als ich will"). The distance of this second point of sight is thus set with absolute arbitrariness. Having indicated his second point of sight he says that he draws lines from it to the points *g* and *f*. (He actually only draws the line to the point *g*.) This done he says that he draws a perpendicular line *aa bb*, which touches the near corner ("die das forder eck an rurt"), that is, at *f*, but which in his diagram actually stands off to the right of *f*. Finally from the point *cc*, where this perpendicular cuts the line between the second point of sight and the point *g*, he draws a transverse line parallel to the line *g f*. At the points where this line cuts the lines from the near point of sight to *g* and *f* he puts the letters *h* and *e*. The line *he* is the missing fourth side of his projected square.

In proceeding in this way Dürer sets off his second point of sight "so weyt als ich will," but without saying from what point its distance was measured off, whether from the near point of sight or the point *f*. It is important

to notice that he sets off this second point of sight before he erects any perpendicular. This would have been in accordance with Alberti's method of procedure within the confines of his box with its fixed, constant positions of eyehole and checkerboard, its shifting, variable position of slide or templet, and the variable size and position of the picture on the slide. But it was wrong when working on a piece of paper, as Dürer did, with shifting, variable positions of eye and checkerboard, and constant position of the picture plane at the near edge of the checkerboard. If Dürer measured the second point of sight off from the near point of sight, then his perpendicular, far from being of any help to him, was only a very disturbing element of confusion and error, because when the construction is based on the distance between the two points of sight, the true geometrical diagram is that shown in figure 21, which is the construction of Viator and contains no perpendicular. If he measured his distance off from the point *f*, he would have had to use one or the other of two ways of carrying that distance up to the central line (which Dürer actually omits) from the ground line, on which the point *f*

36

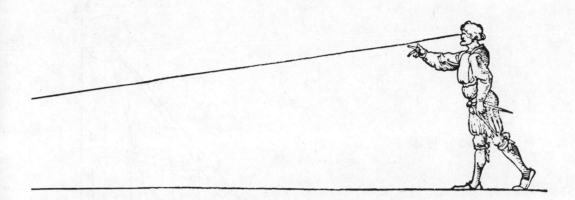

DIAGRAM 59

lies. He could have drawn a perpendicular through the point f and taken his measurement from the point at which the perpendicular cut the central line, as in figure 31. But

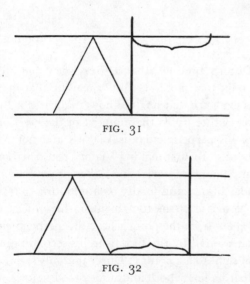

FIG. 31

FIG. 32

this he did not do, because he located his second point of sight before he erected his one perpendicular. The only other way was to measure his distance from the point f along the ground line and then transfer it to the central line by erecting another perpendicular

that cut the central line at the proper place, as in figure 32. But this form of construction requires two perpendiculars, a first one to determine the position of the second point of sight, and then another through the point f, to be used in determining the height of the fourth side of the projected square. As Dürer's description and his diagram contain only one perpendicular it is obvious that his construction was not made in this way.

Further than this it is interesting to note that Dürer did not in fact draw his one perpendicular through the point f but off to one side of it (in a position which logically should have required the drawing of the line, omitted by Dürer in his sketch, from the second point of sight to the point f) ; and that he put the feet of his observer on the lower transverse line (the ground line) instead of on the plane of his square surface, and thereby introduced two unrelated ground lines into his diagram. As part of this last error he made the lower left-hand corner of his construction like figure 34, when, if he had really wanted to put his two points of sight at the same height above his original ground line, it should have been like figure 35. Each of these several things in-

37

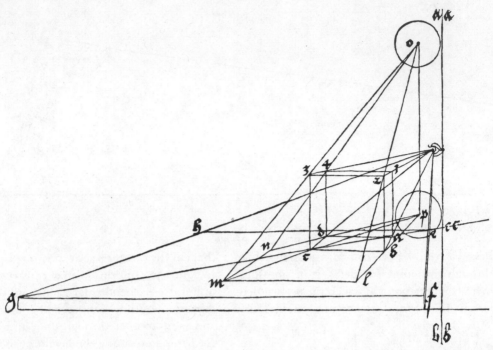

FIG. 33. DÜRER'S

troduced the gravest error into his final results.

As Dürer's only perpendicular was erected after the placing of his second point of sight,

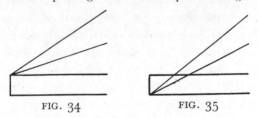

FIG. 34   FIG. 35

it is fair to assume that when and if he measured the distance of his second point of sight, he measured it from his near point of sight, which was the only point on his lacking central line available for the purpose prior to the erection of any perpendicular.

It is usually said, in spite of the various publications of Viator's method, at Toul, at Strassburg, and even at Nuremberg, during

38

Dürer's lifetime, that Dürer knew nothing about that method. But it may be that here is evidence that he did know about it; for his procedure up to the moment of the erection of his perpendicular is Viator's and not Alberti's. By first making Viator's construction, and then by interjecting Alberti's perpendicular into it, and finally by attempting to take the height of the fourth side of his projected square from the point where this perpendicular was cut by the line from his second point of sight to h's point g, Dürer not only showed that he knew both and understood neither of his predecessors, but introduced a series of errors which goes far to explain the odd architectural perspective of many of his woodcuts and engravings. Without knowing it, by proceeding in this way he shortened the actual distance of his second point of sight from the near side of his square by the distance be-

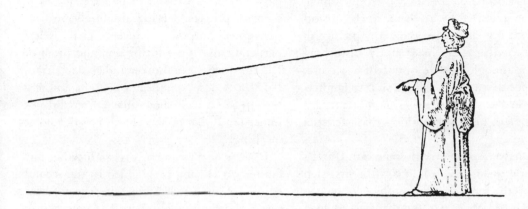

DIAGRAM 61

tween his near point of sight and his perpendicular, and thus succeeded in getting a "photographic wide angle" distortion into his perspective renderings.

If we remember how the minds of schoolboys and other bewildered people work, we get another hint about Dürer's possible knowledge of Viator as well as of Alberti in the fact that in all the constructions in his *Unterweysung* he places his near point of sight very close to his perpendicular. Had he known only Alberti, or only Viator, he would not have needed to do this and could have put his near point of sight out in the middle of his picture where it would have been most useful to him. But, being acquainted with the systems of both his predecessors and understanding neither, he was able to reconcile them only by the expedient of placing his near point of sight as nearly as possible in the one

theoretical position where there was little or no practical difference between them. It happens (see p. 14 above and fig. 36) that when the perpendicular and one of the lines from the near point of sight to the base line coin-

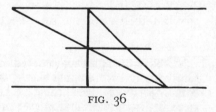

FIG. 36

cide there is no ostensible difference between the constructions of Alberti and Viator. Thus by drawing the constructions in his book with the near point of sight very close to the perpendicular, Dürer played safe in the one general position where the error caused by his confusion of the two systems was the least

39

troublesome. He used this position in many of his woodcuts, and notably in his engraving of Saint Jerome in His Study (B. 60). While this enabled him to satisfy his pedantic yearning for theoretical correctness, it forced him to place his vanishing point away off towards the edge of his picture in a position, which, when emphasized by his "wide angle" distortion, has the effect of making any picture so constructed appear, in a subtly disturbing way, as though it were only half a picture. This peculiarity of construction is so familiar in Dürer's work that it may almost be thought of as one of his distinguishing characteristics as an artist.

We have examined with some care Dürer's diagram 59, in which he takes the first step towards the solution of his problem of how to throw into perspective the shadow cast by a cube resting on a square surface. Let us now pass on to his diagram 61 (our fig. 33), in which he gives his complete answer to the whole problem. This diagram is a cumulative one, purporting to contain all the constructional steps taken from the beginning of the problem to the end of it. In so far as the perspective of the square surface is concerned, therefore, it should be exactly like his diagram 59. But this is not the case, for here

Dürer clearly and definitely throws his square surface into perspective by Viator's method, finding the height of the fourth side of his square by the point where the line from his near eye to the point *f* intersects the line from his second eye to the point *g*. The Albertian perpendicular is there, to be sure, but it is sheer surplusage, serving absolutely no constructional purpose whatever. That useless perpendicular is the fitting sign and proof of Dürer's quality as a thinker and geometrician. It is learned, it complicates matters, and, except in so far as it shows that Dürer did not understand what he was about, it is devoid of meaning.

Dürer's next diagram is reproduced as our figure 37. Having been added to the second edition of his *Unterweysung*, it does not bear one of the running numbers that were cut on the blocks for the first edition. The text of Dürer's explanation of it is given in the facsimile below.[20] In this he purports to tell us how to throw a point into perspective — but, characteristically, he makes a crucial error. In his diagram the picture plane, as determined by the three points, *o*, *a*, and *b*, intersects the ground plane along the axis *a b*, that is, at the side of the square furthest from the observer. To phrase this in terms of our model he has

(20)

Wenn du in einem abgeftolnen planten ein puncten finden wilt/ der dir in eyner rechten fierung fürgeben wirdet/ dem muft alfo than/ Setz ein rechte fierung .a.b.c.d alfo das .a.b. oben zwerchs fey darnach fetz die abgeftolne fierung .a.b.g.f. oben an die ander/ vñ das aug darzu fey .o. dann fetz in die rechte fierung einen puncten .e. wo du hin wilt / darnach reiß in die fierung ein ortftrich .a.c. alfo reiß auch ein gleichmefigen diameter .b.f. in die abgeftolen fierung/ darnach reiß aus dem gegebnen puncten .e. eyn parallel lini gegen oder mit der feitten der fierung biß an die zwerchen .a.b. dahin fetz ein .h. von dann reiß durch die abgeftolen fierung ein gerade lini gegen dem aug .o. biß an die zwerchen .f.g. da fetz ein .m. darnach reiß in der rechten fierung/ ein gerade paralellini aus dem puncten .e. biß an den Diameter .a.c. da hin fetz .ein.i. von dann far mit einer aufrechten parlini biß an die zwerchen .a b. da hin fetz ein .k. von dann reyß zu der abgeftolnen fierung gerad gegen dem aug .o. biß an den ortftrich .f.b. da hin fetz ein .l. von dann far parallel ob .a.b. zwerchs an die lini .h.m. da hin fetz ein .n. Diß ift der gefunden punckt .in der abgeftolnen fierung. vnd ftet gleych meffig in feinem teyl. wie der punckt .e. in der vnderen rechten fierung/ Dife figur hab ich nachfolget alfo auf geriffen.

40

placed his templet at the far instead of at the near side of the checkerboard. In this position of the templet it is impossible by its means to get a perspective image of the square and a point on it except on the supposition that the templet is not a templet but a mirror, in which case the projected image would of necessity be a mirror image, that is, a reversed image. Dürer, however, reverses one of his two diagonal co-ordinates, so that they no longer intersect as they should on the axis of his two planes. By so doing he gets the perspective image *n* of his point *e,* not at the top of the projected square *a b g f,* as it should be in a mirror image, but at its bottom, where it could not possibly be located if his ground and picture planes intersect along the line *a b.* Because of the familiarity of various modern conventions of convenience on the drawing board this is rarely noticed. For Dürer suddenly and knowingly to adopt a factually erroneous convention merely because of its convenience on the drawing board would be completely out of character both for him and for his time. Not only does Dürer nowhere indicate that he is actually resorting to such a convention in the making of this diagram, but such a convention would be in direct conflict with his correct statement in his description of his more complicated method (on leaf ii verso of the 1538 edition of the *Unterweysung*) that his picture plane is a transparent plane, or flat field, which cuts across the lines of sight ("ein durchsichtiger planus oder eben feld der all streymlinien durchschneidet").

The effect of Dürer's misunderstanding of the meaning and use of the perpendicular and

(21) "Sara bene posto questo punto, alto dalla linea che sotto giace nel quadrangolo non più, che sia l'altezza del huomo quale ivi io abbia a dipigniere; pero che cosi et chi vede et le dipinte cose vedute, pajono medesimo in su uno piano." Alberti, Janitschek's edition, p. 79.

the two points of sight was frequently heightened by his failure to obey Alberti's behest to place the center point (or, as Dürer called it, his near eye) at the height of the heads of the figures in the immediate foreground.[21] Far from doing this, he most frequently placed it well above them. This trick or device of a high center point, had Dürer carried it out in

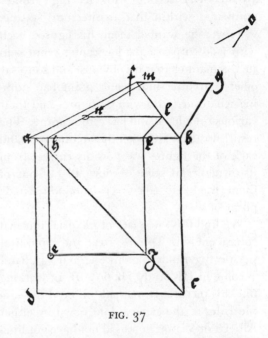

FIG. 37

a logical way, might have produced a point of view much like that utilized on occasion by such a modern master as Degas, but Dürer failed to be logical in his utilization of the high center point. This came about because of his failure to understand that when a picture is made, everything in it, architecture, objects, and figures alike, needs to be represented from one given point of view if the picture is to have any spatial homogeneity.

Analysis of the prints in the Life of the Virgin, including those made both before and after Dürer's Italian trip of 1506–1507, shows that while he habitually used a low center

41

point in sketching his single figures, it was also his habit to use a high center point in sketching or inventing his architecture. From this we learn how he went about building up his compositions. After he had finished his several sketches of the individual figures and of the architecture for a print he copied these sketches off pedantically onto his block — his architectural setting with its high center point and within that architectural setting, wherever he wanted them, his figures, each with its own particular low center point — in such a manner that his obvious, and so to say official, architectural center point had nothing whatever to do with his figures and their various undefined and low center points. The result was that although the architecture and each of the figures was possibly correct from its own special point of view, all but one of them was sadly incorrect from any single point of view.

We find this same lack of pictorial internal cohesiveness in Dürer's great show piece of perspective rendering, his engraving of Saint Jerome in His Study (B. 60). If, in working out this picture, Dürer had followed the simple rules of the game as laid down by either Alberti or Viator, he would not have got himself involved in absurdity after absurdity. The top of the saint's table is of the oddest trapezoidal shape — certainly it is not rectangular. Neither is it level with the floor under it. Moreover, the floor itself is not flat, for somewhere between the table and the bench at its right it takes a sudden tilt and slides off in a new direction. The bench, if a correct projection of it were actually to look like Dürer's picture of it, would have a shape that would astonish everyone, including Dürer himself. These oddities of shape were as carefully disguised or camouflaged by shading as was possible, but anyone who cares to rule lines on a

photograph or reproduction of the engraving will find these and many more to keep them company.

Our analysis of Dürer's perspective theory and practice may perhaps help us to understand how it happens that, no matter what the apparent simplicity and straightforwardness of any of his pictures may be, we are always aware that it contains or is based upon an elusive and tantalizing contradiction. We have seen that his formal perspective construction (the nahere weg) contains logical contradictions. It is obvious from his prints (e.g. the Saint Jerome in His Study, B. 60) that he did not understand that parallel lines in parallel planes meet on the axis of intersection of those planes — a fact that follows immediately out of Alberti's and Viator's constructions. His studies of the proportions of the human body were not based upon anatomy (i.e. upon interior relations) but upon visual shapes in standardized locations (i.e. upon exterior relations). Changes in the locations of his figures within the emphasized and most obvious perspective space of their architectural settings, that is, in their external relationships, were not accompanied by the transformations of their visual (or perspective) shapes that are logically required if their interior relations are to remain invariant through changes in location. These distortions were coupled with the utmost realism in the delineation of forms as seen in locations which they but rarely occupy in his finished pictures. The consistency with which he carried out these various distortions amounts almost to a methodical denial of the homogeneity of space. This fundamental contradiction of one of the great intuitive bases of experience produces a subtle psychological malaise in the beholder of his work that, not being readily traceable to an obvious cause, is doubtless one of the principal reasons for the peculiar fascination that his work has always exercised over the minds of men. It may also be that this basic contradiction is responsible for the fact that so many students of Dürer's work seem always to be working at some conundrum which, like the squaring of the circle, is incapable of solution.[22]

(22) Just as it did not seem necessary to discuss Alberti's famous perspective net so it does not seem necessary to discuss Dürer's even more famous but wholly impractical mechanical aids to perspective. In each instance the basic theory is the important thing and that is set forth in the practical geometrical construction. If the present writer's memory is correct, for it is not a matter to waste time in verifying, the writers who have made most of the nets and other contraptions have also been those who have come to greatest grief in their attempts to explain the geometrical constructions.

BIBLIOGRAPHY

The following list contains the names of a selected few of the books and papers about perspective and geometry that were consulted during the preparation of the foregoing essays. The recent periodical literature is so well summed up in the three important papers marked with an obelus that no other reference is made to it. The history of the history of perspective is so complicated a story of misstatement, misunderstanding, and polemic that, for the sake of simplicity and directness, no references to the "authorities," as distinct from the sources, have been made in the second of the foregoing essays.

GENERAL

Smith, David Eugene. *History of Mathematics.* New York, [1923–1925].

Günther, S., and Wieleitner, H. *Geschichte der Mathematik,* vol. II, part 2. Berlin, 1921. (A good chapter on the history of perspective.)

Cantor, M. *Vorlesungen über Geschichte der Mathematik,* vol. IV. Leipzig, 1908. (Although the standard history of mathematics, its statements about the early history of perspective are to be taken with great caution.)

Enriques, F. *Leçons de géométrie projective.* Paris, 1930. (Especially Appendix VI, an "Aperçu historique et critique sur la genèse des concepts fondamentaux de la géométrie projective.")

Chasles, M. *Aperçu historique sur l'origine et le développement des méthodes en géométrie.* Third edition. Paris, 1889.

Poudra, M. *Histoire de la perspective.* Paris, 1864. (Some of its summaries are still valuable.)

Schonflies, A., and Tresse, A. "Géométrie projective." In *Encyclopédie des sciences mathématiques pures et appliquées,* tome III, vol. II. Paris, 1913.

Enriques, F. "Principes de la géométrie." In *Encyclopédie des sciences mathématiques pures et appliquées,* tome III, vol. I. Paris, 1911.

Baker, H. F. *Principles of Geometry,* vol. I. Cambridge, 1929.

Cremona, L. *Elements of Projective Geometry.* Third edition. Oxford, n.d.

Russell, B. A. W. *An Essay on the Foundations of Geometry.* Cambridge, 1897.

Nicod, J. *Foundations of Geometry & Induction.* London, 1930.

Taylor, Charles. "Geometrical Continuity." In *The Encyclopaedia Britannica.* Eleventh edition, vol. XI, p. 674. New York, 1910.

Whitehead, A. N. "Axioms of Geometry." In *The Encyclopaedia Britannica.* Eleventh edition, vol. XI, p. 730. New York, 1910.

Mach, E. *La Connaissance et l'erreur,* chapters XIX and XX. Paris, 1908.

Heath, Sir Thomas. *A History of Greek Mathematics.* Oxford, 1921.

†Richter, G. M. A. "Perspective, Ancient, Mediaeval and Renaissance." In *Scritti in onore di Bartolomeo Nogara.* Rome, 1937. (An excellent discussion of classical perspective with a valuable bibliography.)

†Wieleitner, H. "Zur Erfindung der verschiedenen Distanzkonstruktionen in der malerischen Perspektive." *Reportorium für Kunstwissenschaft,* vol. XLII (1920), p. 249. (With a most useful bibliography of the periodical literature.)

RENAISSANCE WRITERS ON PERSPECTIVE AND COMMENTARIES ON THEM

Alberti, L. B. *Kleinere Kunsttheoretische Schriften* (text, translations, and notes by H. Janitschek) *(Quellenschriften für Kunstgeschichte)*. Vienna, 1877.

———— *La Pittura* (translated by D. Domenichi). Mondovi, 1565.

———— *Opuscoli morali* (edited by Cosimo Bartoli). Venice, 1568.

———— *De la statue et de la peinture* (translated and edited by Claudius Popelin). Paris, 1868.

Lionardo da Vinci. *Das Buch von der Malerei* (edited by H. Ludwig) *(Quellenschriften für Kunstgeschichte)*. Vienna, 1882. (The note on Alberti in vol. III, pp. 176 ff.)

†Wolff, G. "Zu Leon Battista Albertis Perspektivlehre." *Zeitschrift für Kunstgeschichte*, vol. v (1936), p. 47. (With a critical bibliography of the more recent discussions of Alberti's text.)

Olschki, Leonardo. *Geschichte der neusprachlichen wissenschaftlichen Literatur*. Heidelberg, 1919. (Chapter on Alberti.)

Ravaisson-Mollien, C. *Les Manuscrits de Léonard de Vinci, Le Manuscrit A de la Bibliothèque de l'Institut*. Paris, 1881.

Piero della Francesca. *Petrus Pictor Burgensis de Prospectiva pingendi . . . veröffentlicht von Dr. C. Winterberg*. Strassburg, 1899.

Panofsky, E. *Die Perspektive als "Symbolische Form."* In *Vorträge der Bibliothek Warburg, 1924–1925*, p. 258. Leipzig and Berlin, 1927.

Viator (Jean Pelerin). *De artificiali perspectiva*. Toul, 1505.

de Montaiglon, A. *Notice historique et bibliographique sur Jean Pelerin dit le Viateur*. Paris, 1861.

Dürer, A. *Underweysung der Messung*. . . . Nuremberg, 1525 and 1538.

Panofsky, E. *Dürers Kunsttheorie*. Berlin, 1915.

Hirschvogel, A. *Ein aigentliche . . . anweysung in die Geometria*. [Nuremberg], 1543.

Serlio, Sebastiano. *Il primo libro d'architettura*. Paris, 1545.

Rivius, G. H. *Der furnembsten, notwendigsten, der gantzen Architectur angehörigen Mathematischen und Mechanischen Künst*. . . . Nuremberg, 1547.

Cousin, Jean. *Livre de perspective*. Paris, 1560.

Lautensack, H. *Des Circkels und Richtscheyts, auch der Perspectiva, . . . underweisung*. . . . Frankfort, 1564.

de l'Orme, Philibert. *Le Premier Tome de l'architecture*. Paris, 1567.

Barbaro, Daniel. *La pratica della perspettiva*. Venice, 1568.

du Cerceau, J. A. *Leçons de perspective positive*. Paris, 1576.

Danti, Egnatio. *Le due regole della prospettiva pratica*. Rome, 1583.

Romano, Bartolomeo. *Proteo militare*. Naples, 1595.

del Monte, Guidobaldo. *Montis perspectivae libri sex*. Pesaro, 1600.

LATER WRITERS ON PERSPECTIVE

Bosse, Abraham. *Manière universelle de Mr. Desargues pour pratiquer la perspective*. Paris, 1648.

Desargues, G. *Oeuvres de Desargues réunies et analysées par M. Poudra*. Paris, 1864.

Tannery, P. "Desargues." In *La Grande Encyclopédie*, vol. XIV, p. 203. Paris, n.d.

Monge, G. *Géométrie descriptive*. Paris, An VII; and M. Solovine's edition. Paris, 1922.

Poncelet, J. V. *Traité des propriétés projectives des figures*. Paris, 1822.

Deneux, H. *La Métrophotographie appliquée à l'architecture*. Paris, 1930.

SUPPLEMENTARY BIBLIOGRAPHY (1973)

EARLY EDITIONS OF
DE ARTIFICIALI PERSPECTIVA

First edition: Toul, Pierre Jacobi, July 9, 1509.

Second edition: Toul, Pierre Jacobi, March 4, 1509.

Third edition: Toul, Pierre Jacobi, September 1, 1521.

Pirated editions: *Von der Kunstperspectiva* (with a brief text in German based on the 1505 Toul edition). Nürnberg, Jörg Glockendon, 1509; Nürnberg, Nicolas Glockendon, n.d.; Nürnberg, Albrecht Glockendon, 1540.

Introductio Architectura et Perspectivae. Based on Viator and inserted in Gregor Reisch, *Margarita Philosophica*, Strassburg, Grüninger, 1508, 1512, 1515, 1535, 1583.

ADDITIONAL WRITERS ON PERSPECTIVE

Brion-Guerry, L. *Jean Pèlerin Viator, sa place dans l'histoire de la perspective*. Paris, 1962

Panofsky, Erwin. *Albrecht Dürer*. Princeton, 1945, pp. 242–284.

Rupprich, Hans. *Dürers Schriftlicher Nachlass*. Berlin, 1956–.

Schuritz, H. *Die Perspektive in der Kunst Dürers*. Frankfurt, 1919.

Steck, Max. *Dürers Gestaltlehre der Mathematik und der bildenden Künste*. Halle, 1948.

Viator

DE ARTIFICIALI PERSPECTIVA

Toul, 1505

✝ ·DE·ARTIFICIALI·P SPECTIVA·

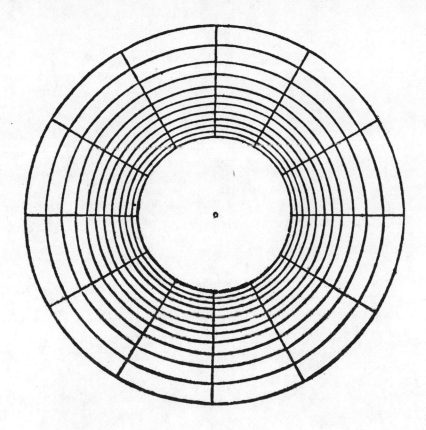

·VIATOR ✝

A t.

De perspectiua positiua: Cõpendiũ.

A fundamentis edificatum iri. Mox sensim extruendum corpus. & tectum imponendũ. Etenim (quod philosophicis spe-
culationibus perspectum est) omnes res videntur tanĝ per
lineas ab oculo egredientes: scilicet p triangulũ. Cui⁹ basis est res visa: eiusĝ diameter super partes ipsius rei vise discurrit. Sed lux ab
oculo non egreditur: verum ex lucis exterioris splendore in oculum ca
dẽte/ sit reflexio quasi a speculo ignito: per quam forme rerum conci-
piũtur. Quarũquidem formarum designatiua expressio/ deriuatur a
puncto. Qui licet indiuiduus sit: euoluitur tamen & in lineam ac lineas explicatur. Ex quibus figure componuntur: per quas/ cum punctis et lineis huiusmodi/ via ad propositum aperitur.

Punctus principalis in perspectiua debet ad normam oculi costi-
tui: qui punctus/ dicitur fixus vel subiectus. Deinde linea produci
ad vtranĝ partem: et in ea duo alia puncta/ eque distancia a subiecto
signari: propiora in presenti/ et remotiora in distanti visu: que dicimĕ
tertĸa puncta. Possunt eciam fieri in ipsa linea alia puncta: vbi apparatus edificii plurium ãgulorum/ vel aliud quid situ diuersum/ occur-
rerit. Dicitur autem piramidalis: quia anguli seu acies piramidũ (de
quibus postea dicetur) ex punctis in ea signatis deducuntur. Vocatur
eciam orizontalis: quia solem oriẽtẽ ostendit/ et occidẽtem abscondit.
Et semper equat oculum hominis vbicũĝ fuerit: eciam si turrim ex-
celsam ascenderit/ vel supercíliũ montis. Ad quam quoĝ altitudinẽ/
extremitas/ seu terre/ siue maris/ debet semper terminari. Nisi altio-
res intermedii montes fuerint obiecti.

Deinde alia inferior linea statuẽda est/ que terrea dicitur: & in ea
(si edificiũ supererigi/ vel dimensionis ratio concipi pretendaĸ)

C. ii.

puncta partita/cum circino apte aperto/disponi: plura vel paucioza: secundum opoztunitatem propositi. Interagēdum etiam aliis pūctis apparatui rerum necessariis/vtendum erit:que hic non designantur sed manifestabuntur per figuras.

PLures quoqȝ alie ducende sunt linee: quarum omnes/a punctis in linea piramidali constitutis exeuntes/generaliter dicūtur radiales:quia procedunt ab ipsis/tanquā radii a sole vel stellis. Specialiter tamē/laterales piramidum/nominantur visuales:subiectum in perspectiua denotantes:et earū medie diametrales. Linee vero commissuris seu adunationibus edificiozum deseruientes/seu directe siue perpendiculares:non habent alia superaddita nomina.

FIgurarum autem:alie ponuntur pro elementis: alie pro exemplis/seu inductiuis: Sed hic primū/de his que pro elementis habentur/sit mētio. Que omnes/a sperica/tanȝ a matre/oziginem trahunt: Nam trigonus/ȝ tetragonus (qui maxime perspectiue deseruiunt)ab ea deducūtur: seu per eam iustificantur. A trigono quid/piramides procedunt: que etiam pire ignis similitudinem przeferunt: late deozsum/ȝ sursum acute. Et possūt singule fieri latiozes/vel azctiozes: longiozes vel breuiozes: Alieqȝ figurari pro exigētia operum. Nam iacenti a dextris fit contraria a sinistris:et pendenti similiter. Omēs tamen quocūqȝ modo fiant cōcurrunt/ et inuicem (sicut littere) operantur:earumqȝ anguli seu acies/ex punctis in linea piramidali assignatis oziuntur. Excepta acie piramidis penultimo loco subsignate que a puncto in aerem coniecto deducitur. Si quas autem aliunde deduci opoztebit:rerum fingendarum speculatio docebit. Prima autem figura/trigonus/vel triāgulus dicitur. Secunda/piramis recta. Tercia/euersa. Quarta iacēs. Quinta/duplex. Sexta/diffusa. Septima/bicoznis vel coznuta. Octaua pendens vel inclinata. Nona (de qua

premiſſum eſt)aerea. Decima/tetragonus vel tetrangulus. Per quẽ
ſpacia depingenda diſponenda ſunt: Aut pauimento limitato/aut(ſi
reb⁹ fingẽdis vel ozdiationi earũ neceſſariũ fuerit)diſtãciis diſcretis.

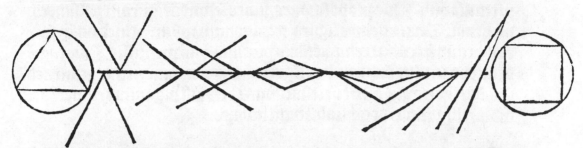

Œterum/diuerſitas aſpectuum rerum obiectarũ ſemper cõſide-
randa eſt:pzeſertim edificiozum. Nam aut viſuntur a frõte:aut
ab angulo. Equilateraliter:vel inequilateraliter. Ex cõmuni:aut eleuata ſede. Et(ſicut pzetactum eſt)de pzeſenti:aut diſtanti viſu. In per-
ſonis quoqʒ in eiſdem ſtatuendis/adequanda eſt quantitas earum/ad
magnitudinem ipſozum edificiozum: vt ſingula rite quadzẽt/ et indu-
ſtriam artificialem redoleant.

Adhuc notandum eſt/ɋ res ſiue magnitudo viſibilis(que eſt ma
teria huius artis) quandoqʒ aſpicitur/vt ab integro cõcipiatur:
et tunc diameter piramidis ſeu trianguli viſualis cadit ex directo ſup
ipſam rem. Nõnunɋ aſpicitur/vt pars aliqua attentius intueatur:et
tunc diameter piramidis ad ipſam partẽ conuertitur. Quemadmodũ
acus hozologii(quod quadzantẽ vocant)ſi lapis magnes circunducaɫ.
Huius pzopoſiti exemplum patet per tetragonum pzimo ſuppoſitũ:
erectum quidem/ et eleuatũ: quem qui totum ſimul aſpexerit pzioris
pzopoſiti argumẽtum tenebit. Qui autem ad coznu ſeu angulum dextrum inflexerit oculum:illic virtus viſiua trãſferet piramidis diametrum. Qui vero adleuum reflexerit ſimiliter.

Inozatio autem tetragoni ſtrati cõpzehenditur per lineas viſuales a pũcto ſubiecto ſuper inferiozes ſeu pzoximos eiuſɔ angu-
los cadentes: et per ſectiões diametroʒ piramidarũ inclinatarũ/pzo-
tenſarum a terciis pũctis duplo a ſubiecto remotis/vel amplius/aut

A iii.

etiam minus/secundum sedem fingentis: et præsentem aut diſtantem
viſū. Circulus vero qui circa tetragonū erectū extat ſpericͦ/circa ſtra-
tum ſit oualis/aut lenticularis/ſecundū differentias ſedium/et viſuū
præmiſſoͣum. Que propoſitiones/ſuper ſecundā figuram poſſunt cō-
præhendi. Tercia deinde figura/tetragonum ipſum ͦtinet/abſcͨ ſpe-
rali circumferentia: remanētibus piramidibus præmiſſis. Que tamē
deinceps in aliis ſequentibus figuris/non ponentur in integrum: ſed
id ſolum ex eis quod erit neceſſarium. Licet ſuffingantur ſemper/vel
ſubintelligantur: vt conſtabit intuentibus.

Dimiuntio quocͨ pauime nti/accipitur ſuper huiuſmodi tetra-
gonum/pūctis partitum/et lineis radialibus diſtinctum/a ſec-
tiͦibus diametroͣum piramidarū inclinatarum/ſicut præmiſſum eſt:
vt quarta quinta et ſexta figuris cum quatuoͣ ſequētibus pluribus
modis oſtenditur. Et poſſunt fieri alia diuerſa pauimēta et multipli-
cari ac dilatari ad placitum. Dͦ qui planiciei campeſtris ſpacia
dimimiere voluerit: protractis lineis rectis pauimēti ſuffiˉcti intentū
habebit. Niſi alia geometrali induſtria id facere pernouerit. Quā-
titas vero ſeu minoͣatio perſonarū: duobus modis accipitur. aut eˉ
ex cōmuni: aut ex eleuata ſede conſpiciuntur. Si ex ſede cōmuni: a ſitu
pedum earum capiuntur: et linea piramidali. Quam eciam lineam
perſone huiuſmodi poſſunt a luminibus ſurſum excedere: vel āplius
in procerioͣe aut gigātea magnitudine. Si ex eleuata ſede: vtendū
eſt inclinata piramide a puncto ſubiecto vel altero ex terciis exeunte:
cuius latitudo baſis aperiatur ad altitudinem proxime ſeu maioͣis
perſone in ſpacio ſtatuende: ſecundum cuius piramidis inarctationē
perſone huiuſmodi a plantis ad ſumma capitum accipiēt miˉ ͣati-
onem: Quarū triū propoſitionū ponūtur exempla per tres figuras
ſequentes pauimenta. Ex quibus figuris nouiſſima ordinaˉ ſecundū
ſedem paulum eleuatāˉ tantum que tamē altius poteſt eleuari: eciā
ſuperel euari: et linea oriͣontalis ac acies piramidis inclinate ſimul
inaltari/prolongari ue aut dilatari vt prenotatū eſt in articulo de figuris elementaribus: prout et plane compͣehendetur ab intentis ſpe-
culatoͣibus. Obicuncͨ autem pueri vel adoleſcētes erunt fingendi:

pro etatibus singuloꝝ venięt in ꝓtitate altitudinis metiendi: Quib⁹
pueris/ceterisꝗ vbilibet assignatis psonis/proportiones legitime da/
buntur pro magnitudinibus suis. Et quod de personis per omnia di/
citur:de ceteris animantibus similiter intelligitur.   Porro:diminu
tio latitudinis colūnaꝛū/et similium rerum/accipiꝗ ex diminutionib⁹
tetragoni/supereleuatis/tamꝗ a basi/colūnis et rebus huiusmodi.
Altitudines vero/constant per piramides oportunas: iacętes scilicet
aut pendentes/secundum earumdem colūnarum sublimitatem/et vi/
dentis sedem.   Sed hoc aduertendum est/ꝗ in visu multum distāti
seu longinquo:expedit sepenumero vti industria et ingenio. Similiꝗ
et in multis aliis/speculationi argutioꝝ relictis.

PRoinde(supradictis ad effectum pretentum plane susceptis) fi/
gure exęplares ad īductiuā descripte videātur.Quarū nōnulle/
ex memoria ꜱtructurarum/ꝗ picturarum quandoꝗ visarum.Alie/ex
ipsa speculatione sunt erecte. Que concipiętur per elemęta premissa/
tamꝗ per litteras verba; Quinpotius/super huiusmodi figuris/in
telligentur eoꝛumdem elementoꝛum officia: quoniam videlicet/pla/
nis formis ꜱtatuendis(a quibus edificia huiusmodi exurgunt)ꝗ rebus
effingendis/ ac cōmissuris/ seu adunatiōibus earum/manuductiuam
habent aptitudinem. In figuris quidem edificioꝛum a fronte conspec/
toꝛum/piramis recta pauimentū constituit:ꝗ due vel plures hincinde
iacentes latera seu parietes:Euersa vero testudinem aut tectum de/
super.In edificiis quoꝗ ab angulo conspectis diffusa et bicoꝛnis ope/
rantur:duplex in vtrisꝗ:pendens pluribus rebus:aerea nonnullis
gradibus ponendis deseruit. Cetera videbuntur experimento ip/
sarum figurarum:In quibus tamen proportiones particulares per/
sonarnm/non obseruātur precise:sed ꝗtitates magnitudinū maxime:
que/ad propositum faciunt. Nec edificia protrahuntur aut variantur
ad omnem plenitudinem:propter spacioꝛum angustias/et faciloꝛem
conceptum artis. ꝗ operis:Operisquidem non pictoꝛis sed pictoꝛum
et artificum atꝗ omniū amatoris: Qui/querentibus perspectiue ex/
orbia qualia ex libꝛis/ꝗ designationibus ac oꝛaculis peritissimoꝛum/
                                                    A iiii.

addita excercitatione conſequi potuit: fines leucoꝝ pertranſiens/pꝛo
mere voluit. Pꝛeter que/multa ſunt et artis/et nobilis pingendi ſub
tilitatis archana: longa eruditione doctioꝛū et actuali rerum natura
lium atꝗ artificialiū contuitu/et permenſa obfiguratiōe exquiꝛenda.
Sculptoꝛum autem nondum tritoꝛum: ipſiusꝗ pꝛotrahentis ſextam
decadem percurrētis omiſſa/vel minus exploꝛata/dirigant videntes:
leni peniculo per ficientes omnia: Ad laudem ſummi artificis dei pa
tris: et filii: ꝗ ſpiritus ſancti. Qui ad perſpiciendam regiam gloꝛioſiſ
ſime maieſtatis ſue/perducat oīes pacificos viatoꝛes terre: Jn qua
ſicut patres noſtri/aduene ſumus/et Peregrini.

Pꝛo cūctis oꝛat fictoꝛ ſcriptoꝛꝗ libelli

Cunctoꝛū pariter ſupplicat ipſe pꝛeces.

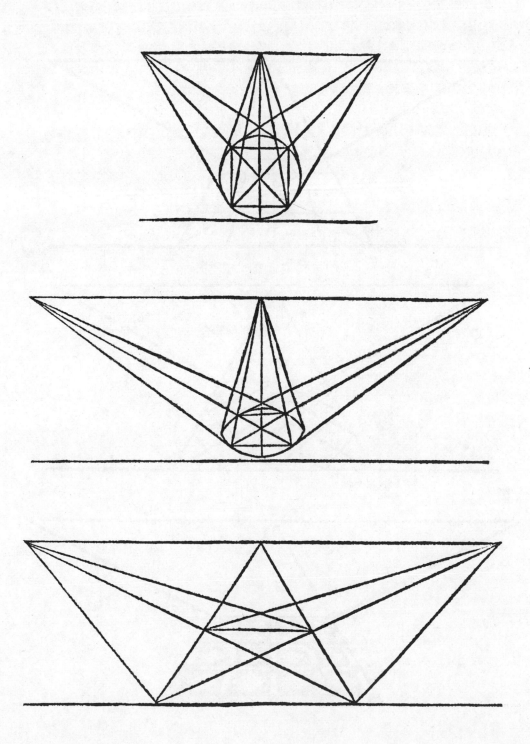

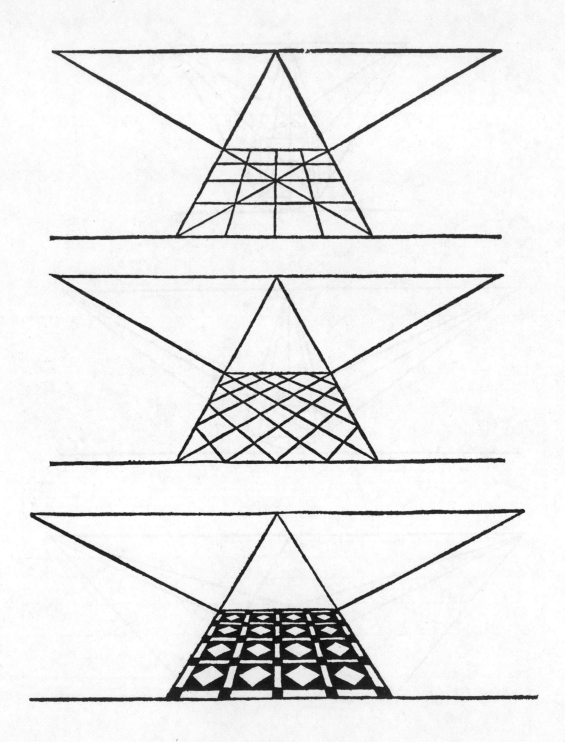

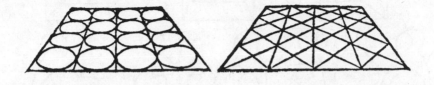

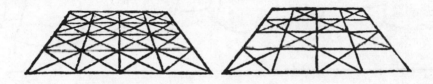

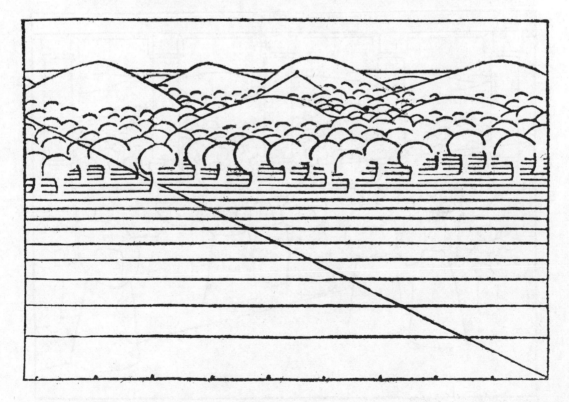

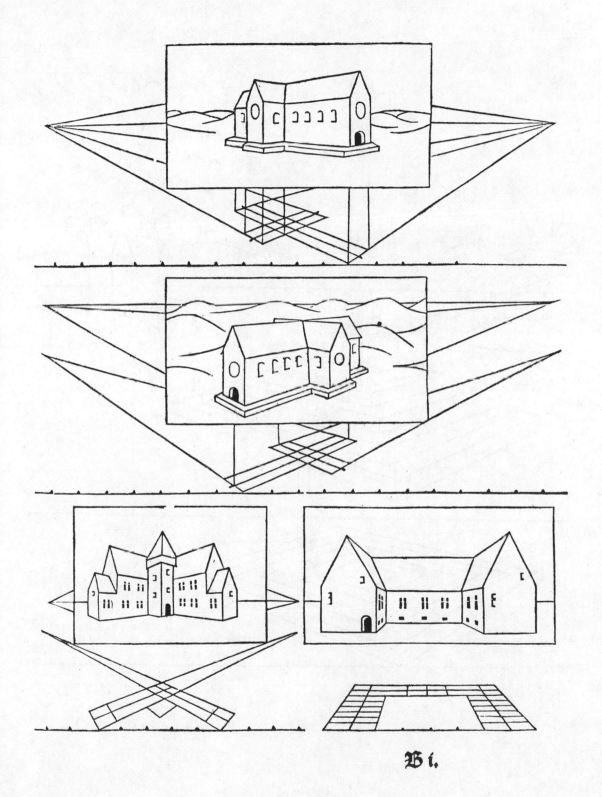

$\mathfrak{B}\,\mathfrak{i}.$

B ii.

B iii.

𝕴𝕴𝕴 i.

A ii.

C iii.

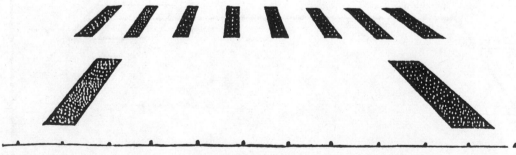

C iiii.

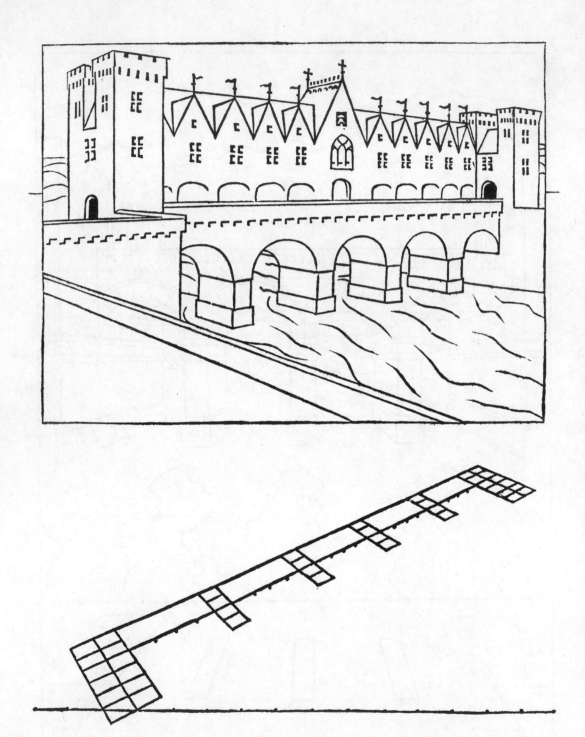

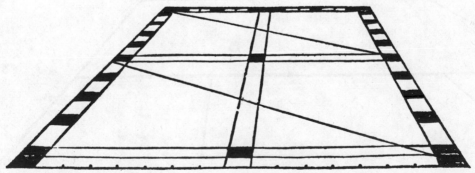

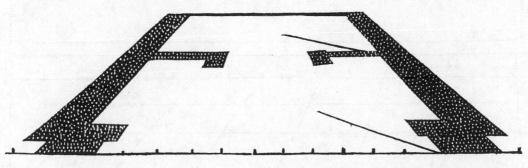

Di.

IV·II
P·M

D ii.

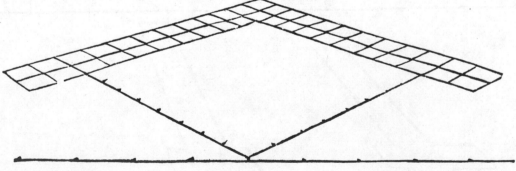

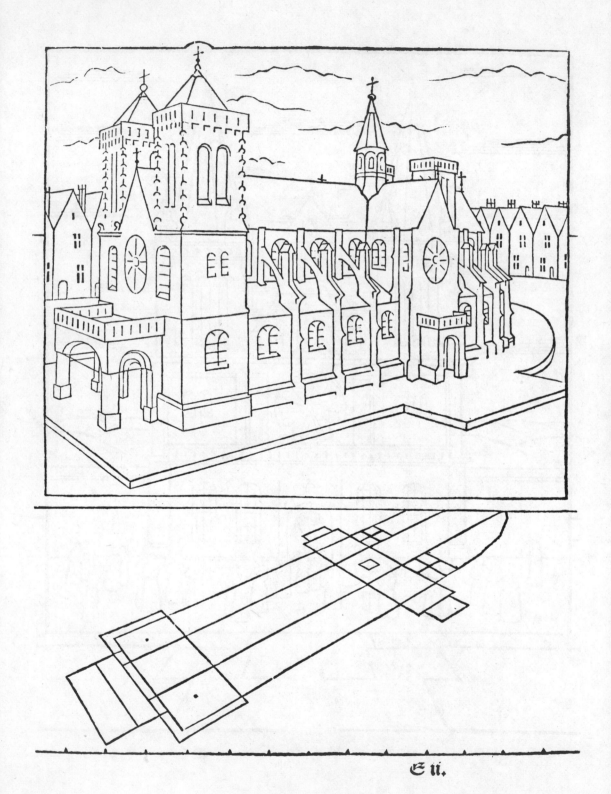

Memoria montis balsami: rupis asperrime: loci penitencie beate marie magdalene.

E iii.

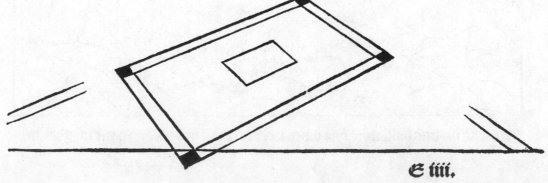

E iiii.

CARRETA·PELEGRINA *

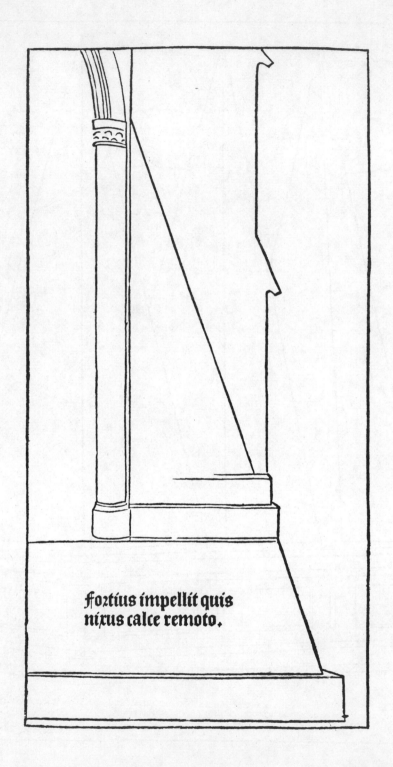

fortius impellit quis
nixus calce remoto.

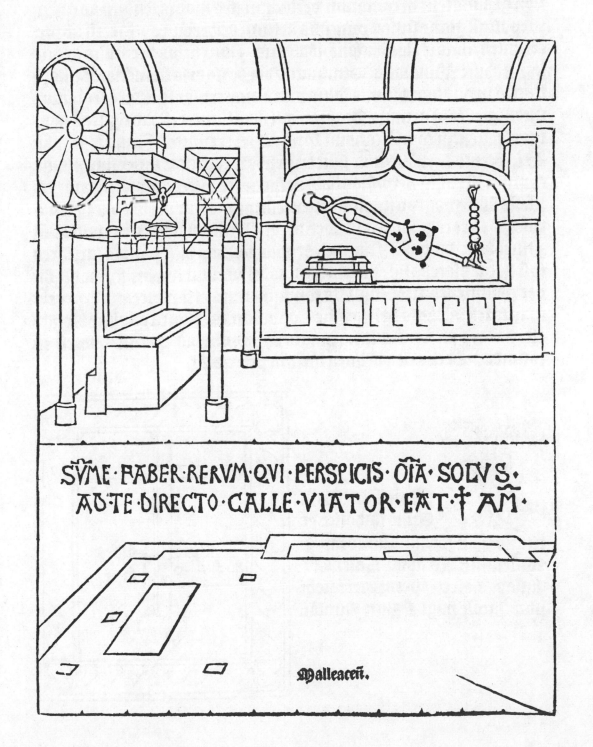

SVME · FABER · RERVM · QVI · PERSPICIS · OĨA · SOLVS ·
AD·TE · DIRECTO · CALLE · VIATOR · EAT † AM̂ ·

Malleaceñ.

Habes optime lectoz de perspectiua positiua perfacile cõpendiũ/
figuris et exemplis appositis multipliciter attestatum. Jn quo
non grauitatem vel oznatum verbozum/sed magis sensum ad finem
pzepositũ(glozie scilicet pzincipis artificũ dei)requiras. Hec tñ ad pze/
cedentiũ maiozē elucidationē addideris. Nam in his pzemissis articu/
lis/Adhuc: Minozatio: Diminutio/vbi de figuris sit mēcio/de illis(q̃
statim in quatuoz vltimis foliis pzimi quaternionis litterã sequũtur)
intellige:At in articulo Pzoinde(qui nouissimus est)ad figuras qua/
tuoz sequentiũ complicationũ B:C:D:E: remitte. Quarũ Jn folio
B i. cõtente/demõstratiue sunt erigendoz. edificioz. super suis planis
fozmis: Relique uero/suas habent speciales differētias/et partim ex/
pzesse sunt/pzout ad manus deuenerũt:ne putetur in eis ozdo necessa/
rius. Sed et regulam (quã liber vocat Nozmam) artifices galli dicũt
Niueolam/vulgarit Niueau/Et quas fozmas dicit planas/ artifices
ipsi vocãt plateas siue platas fozmas. Ozdiũtur autem fozme hmõi/
per pauimenta rite designata/ annumeratis et consideratis super eis
spaciis seu dictātiis vel mensuris oppoztunis. figura oualis oblonga
est/ instar oui. Lenticularis magis appzopínquat sperali/non est tñ
rotunda. Sectio est vbi linea lineam pertransit.

Mpzessum Tulli
Anno catholice ve-
ritatis Quigētesimo quĩto supza
Milesimũ: Ad nonũ Calendas
Julias. Solerti opera petri iacobi
pbzi/Jncole pagi Sancti Nicolai.

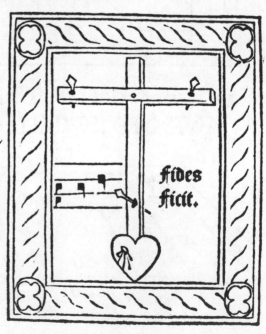

fides
ficit.

LEuure deuant mis parfait/et veu par aucuns: leur a semble estre reqs le transcrire et interpreter en vulgar: affin que les non clers/ puissent aussi entendre le contenu: Et oultre/ que pluseurs diront/que les personnes (qui ne sont que grossemēt esformees)deussent auoir estre entierement pourtraites: Surquoy/au premier point/ pour la cause dite/ est satisfait cy apres: Et quant au scd touchant les personnes/ est assauoir/ que ainsi ont este faites et laissees en bosse ou similitude tant seulemēt/de industrie et certai ppos. pour plusfacile comprehension de lartifice: car lintētion du liure nest/ que de adapter es edifices ou espaces designez en icellui/ou autres telz que lon volra/ les grandeurs & minorations en distance desd personnes: (cōme il est touchie en larticle Proinde/ vers le meilleu.)et nō point de former particulierement.lesd psonnes. Laquelle formatiō/et ceste partie de perspectiue/ont diuerses consideratiōs/ successiuemēt et lune apres lautre itelligibles:(dōt ceste doit estre premier cōceue. Et par ainsi(des querās les pricipes de la matiere(car les doctz et expers ne sout a enseigner/mais fait a aprendre deulx) cue labitude de la maniere proposee la poesie et designation des lineamens desd personnes/telles ou autres quil plaira/ se peut tousiours comprendre:faire et exprimer/ quant il plaist Laquelle consiste en dimēsions arismetrales et doctrine desd maistres (sicōme autres secrez de lart pictorale (dōt les italz tienent la palme)auec excercice de veue actuel/& obfiguration parmesuree/ ainsi quil est contenu on deuantdit article/ peu deuant la fin. Science de argutz et ingenieux entendemens/que les grans & haulx esperis ont/ tousiours (et meritement) amplecte et magnifie/ensemble les parfaiz artifics dicelle: representans les choses passees & absentes/cōme instantes et presentes:et veues/cognoscibles au premier regart:telles qua retenir les speculans:esleuer et mouuoir corages a vertu et diuine action/admiration/et benediction: solacier et releuer les ēnuyz de la vie humaine/ et autres choses desirables faire & exprimer: finalment(pour reprendre le propos)amables & extimables/cōme aussi touz perspecteurs et operateurs de choses excellentes et dignes.

De perspectiua positiua compendiū
Abregie de perspectiue positiue.

Affundamentis: Quant on veult edifier on cōmence aux fondemens: En apres/ on dresse ou bastist les murailles et corps de ledifice: Et consequemment/on appose le toict et couuerture.Ainsi cōuient faire en la presente matiere: Il fault premier auoir cognoissance des pricipes: Et iceulx entenduz/soy appliqr a la maniere de proceder a besoigner. Et finablement se excercer a pourtraire et figurer artificialmēt les choses veues ou conceues. Quant aux principes/ il est perspect et deduit par speculations de philosophes/ que toutes choses sont veues cōme par lignes procedēs de lueil/ Cestassauoir par le triāgle:du quel labasse est la chose veue:t son diametre discourt/par la motion de lueil/sur les parties dicelle chose veue; Touteffoiz lumiere ne ist pas de lueil: mais la clarte exteriore cheant en icellui/reflecte/comme dun miroir ardent:par quelle reflection les formes des choses sont conceues t apprehendees. Desquelles formes/la designatiue et figu/ ratiue expression/est deriuee du point: lequel (cōbien que soit indiuidu) est euolue en ligne et en lignes:dont figures sont composees/ par lesquelles/ auec points/et telles lignes/la voye au propos est ouuerte.

Ductus principalis: Le point principal en perspectiue doit estre constitue et assis au nyueau de lueil: lequel poīt est appelle fix/ou subiect.En apres/ vne ligne produite et tiree des deux pars dudit point: et en icelle ligne doiuēt estre signez deux autres points/equedistans du subiect: plus prochains en presente/ et plus esloignez en distant veue:lesquelz sont appellez tiers points. Et en icelle li/ gne peut on faire autres poīts/ ou il estherra apprest de edifice de pluseurs angles/ ou autre chose de diuerse situatiō.Laquelle ligne est appellee piramidale: car les angles ou pointes des piramides (dont cy apres sera dit) sont deduiz des points en icelle constituez. Et est aussi appellee orizontale: car elle mōstre le soleil oriēt/ et le absconde occident:et tousiours adeque en pareille haulteur lueil de lōme/ ou quil monte t se trāsporte: soit a la summite de haulte tour/ou du plus esleue mont qui soit. A quelle haulteur la extremite et de terre/ et de mer/ se doit tousiours ter/ miner: se plus haults monts/entremoyens/ne sont obiectz.

DEinde: En apres/ vne autre ligue plusbasse/ se doit asseoir/ qui sappelle ligne terre:Et en icelle(seon pretend sureriger edifice/ou cōceuor raison de quelque dimension) disposer auec le compas/aptemēt ouuert/poīts partiz:plus/ ou moins: selon lopportunite du propos conceu. Et en besoignāt fault vser dau/ tres points/ necessaires a lapprest des choses:qui ne sont pas cy designez: mais seront manifestez par les figures.

DLures quoqz: Et pluseurs autres lignes sont a tirer: Desquelles toutes yssans des poīts cōstituez en la ligne piramidale/generalmēt sōt appellees radiales.car elles procedent diceulx points/comme les raiz procedent du soleil ou des estoilles. Specialment touteffoiz/ les ligues laterales des piramides/ sont

nõmees visuales: denotãs le subiect en perspectiue: et les moiennes dicelles sapel-
lent diametrales/ cest adire les diuisans en deux pties equales. Quãt aux lignes
seruans aux assemblemens et adunations des edifices/ soient directes ou perpen-
diculaires/ elles nont point autres noms.

Igurarum autem: Quãt aux figures/ les vnes sont mises pour elemẽts/
les autres pour exẽples/ ou inductiues de besoigner en plusgrandes. Mais
cy est faite mencion de celles qui sont mises pour elements. Toutes lesquelles/
procedent de la sperique: Car le triangle/ et le quadrãgle (qui principalmẽt seruẽt
a la perspectiue) sont deduiz et iustifiez par icelle. Duquel triangle procedent les
piramides: qui ont similitude de flãme de feu: large par bas/ et acue en hault: ⁊ se
peuent toutes et chũnes leſõ piramides/ faire pluslarges/ ou plusestroites: plus
longues/ ou plusbreues: et autres figurer/ pour et selon lexigeuce des euuers qnõ
emprendra: Car a la gisaut a dextre/ se fait sa contraire a la senestre: ⁊ semblable-
mẽt a la pendente. Et toutes piramides/ en quelque maniere que soiẽt faites/ cõ-
courent/ ⁊ besoignent ensemble/ cõme les lettres: et leurs angles ou pointes nais-
sent des points assignez en la ligne piramidale: Excepte la pointe de la piramide
signee on penultime lieu: laqlle est deduite dun point coniect en lair. Et sil fault
dailleurs deduire autres piramides/ ce enseignera la speculation des choses quõ
voldra faindre: La premiere figure/ sapelle trigone ou triãgle: la seconde/ piramide droite: la tierce/ euerse: la quarte/ gisant: la quinte/ double: la sexte/ diffuse: la
septime/ bicorne ou cornue: la octaue/ pendente: la neufieme/ aereale: la dixieme/
tetragone ou tetrangle: Par lequel les espaces depingendes/ sont a disposer: ou
par pauement limite: ou (se aux choses quon voldra faindre/ ou a lordonnance di-
celles/ il sera necessaire) par distances discretes.

Eterum. En oultre/ la diuersite des regars des choses obiettes est tous-
tours a cõsiderer: mesmement de edifices. Car on les voit de front/ ou par
langle. Cest adire par deuant/ ou par le coign. ⁊ les peut on veoir equilateralmẽt
ou inequilateralmẽt: et de siege comun/ ou esleue. et (cõme il a este touchie dessus)
de presente/ ou distante beue. Et en statuẽt ou asseant psonnes eſõ edifices/ fault
adequer ou conformer leur quantite a la magnitude diceulx: affin q̃ toutes choses
aptement cõuiennẽt/ et redolent ou representent industrie artificiale.

Dhuc notandum est: Encor est a noter que chose on magnitude visible
(qui est la matiere de cest art) est aucuneffoiz regardee pour estre conceue et

comprife entierement: et lozs le diametre de la piramide ou triangle visual/ chet dzoitement sur icelle chose: Aucunesfoiz est regardee/pour que lune partie soit plusattentement intuite et parueue: et lozs le diametre de la piramide est couerti a icelle partie:côme leguille dun hozologe dit quadzant/se pierre daymant est circumduit. Duquel ppos lexemple appert par le tetragone cy apzes pzemier mis: erect a esleue: lequel qui tout ensemble regardera/ du pzemier pzopos largument et côceptiô tiendza: Et qui au cozne ou angle dextre flectera lueil/ a icelle part/ la vertu visiue trâspoztera le diametre de la piramide. Et q au senestre/peillemêt.

Minozatio autem: La minozation du tetragone/cest adire du quadzangle/ sterne et couchie/ou gisant en plain/se comptêt par les lignes visuales cheans sur les angles dicellui inferiozes et pchains:et par les sectiôs des diametres des piramides inclinees/pzotendues des tiers poîts esloignez du subiect/au double des pzecedês:ou voircint plus/ ou aussi moins que les double/selon le siege du fingent/ et pzesente ou distante veue: et le sercle qui entour le quadzangle erect se demôstre speric/ est a lentour du sterne et gisant/oual/ou lenticulaire:selon la difference des sieges a vcues pzemis.Lesquelles pzopositions se peuent compzendze sur la seconde figure.La tierce consequête figure/contient le quadzangle sans circumference sperale: demozans les piramides pzemises: Lesquelles touteffoiz es autres ensuiuâtes figures ne seront pas entieremêt mises:mais ce seulement dicelles que sera necessaire.Combien que tousiours soiêt sobzfaintes ou sobzentêdues:côme il apperra a ceulx qui y regarderont.

Diminutio quoqz pauimenti: Et la diminution du pauemêt/ se pzent sur les quadzangle/parti de points/ et distinct de lignes radiales/aux sections des diametres des piramides inclinees(côme il est deuant touchie) et plusaplain en maintes manieres demonstre/ par les quarte quinte et sexte figures/auec les quatre sequentes:a se peuent faire autres diuers pauemês/et multiplier a dilater au plasir de louurier. Et qui veult limiter les distâces despace châpestre/en pourtraiant les dzoites lignes de pauement sobzfaint/aura son intencion:se par autre geometrale industrie naura cogneu le faire. Et quant ala minozation des psonnes(dôt les plus esloigneez apperent a lueil/moindzes que les pzochaines) elle est pzinse en deux manieres. Car on les puet regarder de siege commun/ ou de siege esleue.Se on les voit de siege cômun.on pzêt leur haulteur et minozatiô/de leurs piez/a la ligne piramidale:laquelle ligne/les psonnes puêt exceder des yeux en sus:ou plus/ en pzocere et giganteale magnitude:Se on les voit de siege esleue/

fault vſer de la piramide inclinee/yſſant du point ſubget/ou de lun des tiers:de la quelle/la latitude baſſe/ſoit ouuerte a la haulteur de la prochaine et plusgrande pſonne quon voldra ſtatuer en leſpace. ſelon la inarctation de laquelle piramide/ leſd pſonnes prendrõt de la plante au hault des teſtes leur minoration. Deſquelles trois ppoſitions (ceſtaſſauoir de limiter eſpaces champeſtres: et de aſſeoir et minorer les quantitez de pſonnes veues de ſiege cõmun/ et auſſi de ſiege eſleue) les exemples apperent par les trois figures ſupuans les pauemens. Dont/ la derreniere eſt ordonnee/ſelon ſiege peu eſleue/ et ſe puet eſleuer plushault/ et encores ſureſleuer/a la ligne orizontale/ et auſſi la pointe de la piramide inclinee/ enſemble eſleuer/prolonger/ ou dilater: ainſi quil eſt deuant note en larticle des figures elementaires: cõme auec ce ſera cõprins des intens ſpeculateurs. Et en quelque lieu que lon volra faindre enfans ou adoleſcens/ ſera leur quãtite a pren/ dre ſelon leurs aages: eu regart a la quantite des plusgrandes pſonnes: auſquelz enfans/a autres pſonnes/ou que ſoient aſſignees/pportiõs legitimes ſerõt don/ nees ſelon leurs magnitudes. Et ce que par tout eſt dit des pſonnes/ eſt entendu ſemblablemẽt des autres animants./ Et au regart de la diminution de la latitude et groſſeur de cõluneset ſemblables choſes/elle ſe prent par la diminutiõ du tetra/ gone:en ſureſleuãt/cõme delabaſſe/leſd colũnes a choſes:et les haulteurs dicelles/ ſe prenẽt par piramides cõuenables/ Ceſtaſſauoir par les giſantes/ ou pendetes: ſelon la ſublimite deſd colũnez/et le ſiege du voiant icelles. Mais il eſt a auertir/ que en veue moult diſtante et eſloignee/ eſt expedient vſer ſouuenteffoiz de indu/ ſtrie et engin: et ſemblablemẽt/en maintes autres choſes/ laiſſees a la ſpeculatiõ des plusargutz et ſubtilz.

PRoinde: Conſequenmẽt (Les choſes deſſus dites/a leffect pretendu plai/ nement priſes) les figures exẽplaires/deſcriptes a inductiue/ſoiẽt veues: deſquelles aucunes ſont erigees de la memoire de edifices ou paintures aucunes/ foiz et pieca veues: lesautres/de la ſpeculation du diſtant. Leſquelles ſeront cõ/ ceues par les elemẽs premis:cõme ſont parolles par les lettres.Ou mlʳ/ſur icel/ les figures/ſeront entenduz les offices diceulx elemẽs: cõme ilz ont aptitude ma/ nuductiue a ſtatuer les plaines et plates formes/ dont ſont eſleuez leſd edifices et choſes effingibles/a a leurs aſſemblemẽs et adunatiõs. Car es figures veues de plaine frõt/la piramide droite/conſtitue le pauemẽt:a deux ou pluſeurs giſantes/ les coſtez ou paroiz:la euerſe/la volte ou toict deſſus: Et es figures veues angu/ lairemẽt/la diffuſe et la cornue/beſoignẽt:la double/en toutes deux:la pendente/ ſert a pluſeurs choſes: la aerealc/ a faindre aucuns degrez: Le ſourplus ſera veu par lexperiēce dicelles figures. Esquelles touteffoiz les pportions particulieres des personnes ne sont pas precisement obseruees: car cest vne autre maxime speculation/dout cy nest aucunemēt touchie: mais les quantitez de leurs grandeurs signāment/qui sont au propos: et les edifices ne sont pas pourtraiz ne bariez ou enrechiz de fueillages et diuers signes/a toute plenitude/(car maintes choses se mettent en grans volumes/qui sont demozees) pour les petiz espaces/et mesme de industrie ny ont este mis que les principaulx traiz/pour plus facile cōception de lart et de leuure. Lequel euure nest de main de paitre mais de qui aine les paitres et artisans/et touz biuās: qui aux querans les principes de la perspectiue dessusō/quelz il a peu consupz des liures/euures/z ozacles/ ou collatiōs/de tresperitz/passant par les fins de lozraine a bolu et este curieux mettre par escript. Oultre les quelz principes/maints secretz sont de la noble subtilite de painture/a querir par longue erudition de plusdoctz et maistres en la science dite/et par actuel contuit ou regart/ auec parmesuree obsiguration et contrefacture des choses naturelles et artificiales. Ausourplus/les obmissions ou choses moins explozees des sculpteurs 'non encozes tritz ou frotez) et du pourtraiant percurrent la sixieme decade buellēt dzesser les boians: parfaisans le tout au piusceau doulx et gracieux. A la loenge du souuerain artific dieu/pere/filz/ et saint espit Qui a perspicer et contempler la cite roiale de sa souueraine maieste/ bueille conduire touz pacificz biateurs de la terre: eu la quelle cōme noz peres sōmes estraingiers et pelerins:

Pzo cunctis ozat.
Cellui qui a ce liure fait
Pzie pour touz de cueur pfait
Et supplie treshumblement
Pzier pour lui pareillement

Habes optime lecto:: O tresbon lecteur/present as tresfacile ab:egie dela
perspectiue positiue/ acteste en pluseurs manieres de figures et exemples.
Duquel ne requier grauite ou ao:nemēt de paroles/mais plus le sens au fin p:e
pose de la gloire de dieu p:ice des artifics. Toutesfoiz a plusg:āt declaration des
choses p:ecedētes: est a adiouster/car es p:emis articles Adhuc: Mino:atio: Di
minutio: esquelz est faite mencion des figures/entens de celles qui suyuent indi
stāment la lettre/es quatre derreniers fueilletz du p:emier quaterne. Et en lar
ticle P:oinde (qui est le dernier) ou est touchie desō figures/est a entend:e de celles
qui sont cōtenues es quatre quaternes ensuyuans/signez B: C: D: E: desquel
les/ celles qui sont contenues on fueillet B. i. sont demonstratiues de eriger edi
fices sur leurs plates fo:mes: les aults desō quatre quaternes/ont leurs speciales
differences/et en p:tie ont este imp:imees cōme elles sont venues es mais des ou
uriers: affin quō ne pense o:d:e estre necessaire entre icelles. Dultreplus/la rigle
que le liure appelle no:ma/les artisans des gaules dient Niueau. Et les fo:mes
que les liure nomme plaines/ les artisans appellent plates fo:mes: Lesquelles
plates fo:mes sont cōmencees et d:essees par les pauemens aptement pourtraiz/
adnōb:ez et considerez sur iceulx les espaces e distances ou mesures oppo:tunes.
Enquoy faisant est requise intente speculacōn. figure ouale est oblongue/ a la
semblāce dun oeuf. figure lenticulaire/ap:oche plus de la sperale: toutessoiz nest
pas ronde. Section est où vne ligne trespasse lautre.

finis. Laus deo.

Viator
DE ARTIFICIALI PERSPECTIVA
Toul, 1509

✠ DE·ARTIEICIALI·PSPECTIVA·

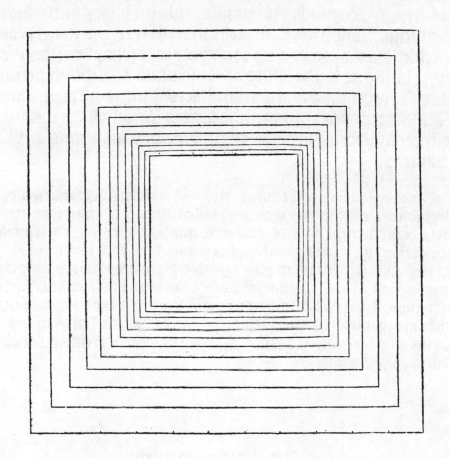

✠ VIATOR : SECVNDO

❡ Pinceaux / burins / acuilles / lices /
Pierres / bois / metaulx / artifices :

A

IN Nomine sūmi opificis. Rogatus ab amicis/et rerū sub=
tilium (& quid optabiliū) studiosis/ Minimus viator trac=
tatum de perspectiua positiua superioribus annis editum
seriosius et apertius exarare: Considerans prouerbiū me=
rito tritum. Bonū/ q̄to cōmunius tanto melius: & dictū/ quo clarius
eo gratius: Cupiensq̄ vniuersis morē gerere/ pariter et prodesse. ac
benedictiones & preces ampliores promouere: opus resumere propo=
suit:et latina ac vulgari lingua/consecutiue rem ipsam percurrere:et
quibusq̄ capitulis proprias familiares figuras. ad expetitam seriem
et ampliorem declarationem facientes. accōmodare curauit: Aliis
postmodum exemplaribus/vnacū breuibus inductiuis. per singulas
subiunctis.

¶ On Nom du souuerai ouurier. Requis damis/et studieux de choses subtiles
et optables/ Le menre des viateurs/plusserieusemēt et ouuertement coucher le
tractie de perspectiue positiue/naguieres mis sus: Considerant le prouerbe me=
ritemēt trit:vng bien de quant est plus cōmun/de tant est meilleur:et vng dit/de
quant est plus cler/de tant est plus agreable:Et desirant faire plaisir et pareille=
ment proffiter a tous/ & promouuoir de plus en plus/benedictiōs et prieres/ A p=
pose resumer leuure: et en latin et vulgar cōsecutiuemēt parcourir la matiere/ et
a chacuns chapitres adapter propres familieres figures/faisans a lordre requis
et plusample declaration dicelle: Subiointes autres exemplaires auec briefz
inductifz par chacune.

¶ Art desperis ingenieux/
Et subtilz/et industrieux/

...fundamentis edificatum iri. Mox sensim extruendu corpus. et tectum imponendu. Eteni (quod philosophicis speculationib9 perspectu est) omnes res videntur tanq̃ per lineas ab oculo egredientes: scilicet per triangulu. Cuius basis e res visa: eiusq̃ diameter / sup partes ipsius rei vise discurrit. Sed lux ab oculo non egreditur: veru ex lucis exterioris splendore in oculum cadente / ut reflexio quasi a speculo ignito: per quã forme reru concipiutur. Quaruquidem formaru designatiua expressio / deriuat a puncto. Qui licet indiuiduus sit: euoluitur tamen / et in lineam ac lineas explicatur. Ex quibus figure componutur: per quas cum punctis et lineis huiusmodi / via ad propositu aperitur.

Quant on veult edifier on commence aux fondemens: En apres / on dresse ou bastist les murailles et corps de ledifice: Et consequentment / on appose le toict et couuerture. Ainsi conuient faire en la presente matiere: Il fault premier auoir cognoissance des principes: Et iceulx entendu3 / soy appliquer a la maniere de proceder a besoigner. Et finablemet se exercer a pourtraire 7 figurer artificialmet les choses veues ou conceues. Quãt aux principes / il est perspect 7 deduit par speculatios de philosophes / que toutes choses sont veues cõme par li gnes precedes de lueil / Cestassauoir par le triãgle: duquel la basse est la chose veue / et son diametre discourt / par la motion de lueil / sur les parties dicelle chose veue: Touteffoiz lumiere ne ist pas de lueil: mais la clarte exterioze cheat en icellui / reflecte / comme dun miroir ardent: par quelle reflection les formes des choses sont conceues et apprehendees. Desquelles / formes / la designatiue et figuratiue expression / est deriuee du point: lequel (combien que soit indiuidu) est euolue en li gne et en lignes: dont figures sont composees / par lesquelles / auec poits / et telles lignes / la voye au propos est ouuerte.

Punctus principalis in perspectiua / debet ad normã oculi consti tui: qui punctus / dicitur fixus vel subiect9. Deinde linea produci ad vtramq̃ partem: et in ea duo alia puncta / equedistancia a subiecto signari: propiora in presenti et remotiora in distanti visu: que dicũtur tercia puncta. Possunt etiam fieri in ipsa linea alia puncta: vbi appa

ratus edificii plurium ãgulorum/vel aliud quid situ diuersum/occur
rerit. Dicitur autem piramidalis:quia anguli seu acies piramidū(de
quibus postea dicetur)ex punctis in ea signatis deducuntur. Vocatur
etiam orizontalis: quia solem oriente ostendit et occidentē abscondit.
Et semper equat oculum hominis vbicūqz fuerit: etiam si turrim ex
celsam ascenderit vel superciliū montis. Ad quam quoqz altitudinē
extremitas/seu terre/siue maris/debet semper terminari. Nisi altio
res intermedii mōtes fuerit obiecti.

LE point principal en perspectiue doit estre constitue z assis au nyueau de
lueil: lequel point est appelle fix/ou subiect. En apres/vne ligne produite
et tiree des deux pars dudit point:et en icelle ligne doiuēt estre signez deux autres
poits/equedistans du subiect:plus prochains en presente/et plus esloignez en di
stante venue:lesquelz sont appellez tiers poits. Et en icelle ligne peut on faire au
tres points/ou il escherra apprest de edifice de pluseurs angles/ou autre chose de
diuerse situation. Laquelle ligne est appellee piramidale: car les angles ou poin
tes des piramides (dont cy apres sera dit) sont deduiz des points en icelle consti
tuez. Et est aussi appellee orizontale:car elle monstre le soleil orient/et absconde
loccident:z tousiours adeque en pareille haulteur lueil de lomme/ou quil monte
et se transporte:soit a la summite de haulte tour/ou du plus esleue mont qui soit.
A quelle haulteur/la extremite/z de terre/et de mer/se doit tousiours terminer:se
plushaults monts/entremoyens/ne sont obiectz.

La. iii.

DEinde alia inferior linea statuenda est que terrea dicitur:et in
ea (si edificiū supererigi/vel dimensiois ratio concipi pretēda
tur) pūcta partita/cū circino apte apto/sūt disponēda: plura vel pau
ciora:secundū oportunitatē propositi. Interagendū etiam/aliis pūctis
apparatui rerū necessariis/vtendū erit:que hic nō designant/sed ma
nifestabuntur per figuras.

EN apres/vne autre ligne plus basse/se doit asseoir/qui sappelle ligne terre:
Et en icelle(se on pretend sureriger edifice/ou conceuor raison de quelque
dimension) fault disposer auec le compas/ aptemēt ouuert/points partiz/plus/
ou mois:selon loportunite du propos conceu. Et en besoignāt fault vser dautres
points necessaires a lapprest des choses: qui ne sont pas cy designez: mais seront
manifestez par les figures.

Plures quoq alie ducende sunt linee:quarum omnes/a punctis in linea piramidali cõstitutis exeuntes/generaliter dicũtur radiales:quia pzocedunt ab ipsis/tanquã radii a sole vel stellis. Specialiter tamẽ laterales piramidum/nominantur visuales/subiectum in perspectiua denotantes:et earũ medie/diametrales.

Et pluseurs autres lignes sont a tircr:Desquelles/toutes ysãs des poits constituez en la ligne piramidale/generalmét sont appellees radiales.car elles pzocedent diceulx points/comme les raiz pzocedent du soleil ou des estoilles. Specialment toutesfoiz/les lignes laterales des piramides/sont nõmees visuales/dxnotans le subiect en perspectiue:et les moiênes dicelles sappellent diametrales/cestadire les diuisans en deur parties equales.

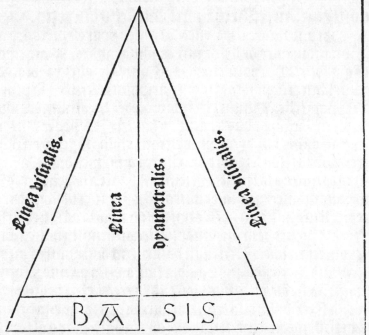

Linee vero commissuris seu adunationibus edificiozum deseruientes/seu directe/siue ppendiculares: nõ habẽt alia supaddita nomina.

Quant aux lignes seruans aux assemblemẽs et adunations dxs edifices/soiét directes ou perpendiculaires/elles nont poit autres noms.

Figurarũ autẽ: alie ponũtur pzo elementis: alie pzo exẽplis/ seu inductiuis: Sed hic pzimũ/de his que pzo elementis habẽtur/ sit mẽtio.Que oĩs/a spherica/tanq a matre ozigirẽ trahunt. Nam trigonus ₹ tetragonus(qui maxime pspectiue deseruiũt)ab ea deducũ: seu per eã iustificant.A trigono quid piramides pzocedũt: que etiam pire ignis similitudinẽ referunt:late deozsum ₹ sursũ acute.Et possũt

singule fieri latiores/ vel arctiores: lõgiores/vel breuiores: Alicq3 figurari pro exigẽtia operũ. Nam iacẽti a dextris/fit cõtraria a finistre
et pendẽti similiter. Oẽs tamẽ quocũq3 modo fiãt/ ̧pcurrũt/ et inuicẽ
(ficut littere)operant̃:earũq3 anguli feu acies/ex pũctis in linea piramidali aſſignatẽoriunt̃. Excepta acie piramidis penultimo loco fub-
ſignate/que a pũcto in aere coniedo deducit̃. Si quas autẽ aliunde deduci oportebit:rerũ fingendarũ fpeculatio docebit.Prima autẽ figura
trigonus/vel triãgulus dicitur. Scõa piramis recta. Tercia/euerfa.
Quarta/iacẽs. Quita duplex. Sexta/diffufa. Septima bicornis vel
cornuta. Octaua/pendẽs vel inclinata. Nona(de qua ̧pmiſſum eſt) a-
erea. Decima tetragonus vel tetrãgulus. Per quẽ fpacia depigenda
difponẽda ſũt:aut pauimẽto limitato/aut(fi rebus fingendis/vel ordi-
nationi earũ neceſſariũ fuerit)diſtãciis difcretis.

QVãt aux figures/les vnes sõt mises pour elemẽts/les autres pour exẽples
ou inductiues de befoigner en plufgrandes. Mais cy eſt faite mention de
celles qui font mifes pour elemẽts.Toutes lefquelles/ ̧pcedẽt de la fpherique:
Car le triãgle/ ̧ le quadrãgle(qui ̧pcipalmẽt feruẽt a la ̧pfpectiue)font deduiz ̧
iuſtifiez par icelle. Duquel triãgle ̧pcedẽt les piramides:qui ont fimilitude de
flãe de feu:large par bas/et acue en hault: Et fe peuẽt touţ et chũnes lefõ pira-
mides/faire plus larges/ou plus eſtroites:plus lõgues/ou plus breues: et autres
figurer/pour ̧ felon lexigẽce des ̧euures quõ ̧eprendra: Car a la gifante a dextre/
fe fait fa cõtraire a la feneſtre: ̧ femblablemẽt a la pendẽte. Et toutes piramides
en quelque maniere que foiẽt faites/ cõcourent/et befoignent enfemble/ cõme les
lettres:et leurs ãgles ou poĩtes naiſſent des poĩts aſſignez en la ligne piramidale
Excepte la poĩte de la piramide fignee on penultime lieu:laͥlle eſt deduite dun
point coniect en lair.Et ſil fault dailleurs ̧deduire autres piramides/ce ̧efeignera
la fpeculatiõ des chofes quõ bouldra faindre:La premiere figure/fappelle trigone
ou triãgle:la fecõde/piramide droite:la tierce/euerfe: la quarte/gifante: la quinte/
double:la fexte/diffufe:la feptieme/bicorne ou cornue:la octaue/pendẽte:la neuf-
ieme/aercale:la dixieme/tetragone ou tetrãgle: Par leͥl les efpaces depigendes/
ſõt a dͥfpofer:ou par pauemẽt limite: ou (fe aux chofes quon bouldra faindre/ ou
a lordõnance dicelles/ il fera neceſſaire) par diſtances difcretes.

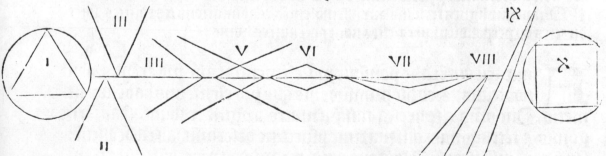

Æterum/diuersitas aspectuum rerum obiectarū semper cōside-
randa est:presertim edificiozū. Nam aut visuntur a fronte:aut
ab angulo.Equilateraliter:vel inequilateraliter. Ex cōmuni: aut cle-
uata sede.Et (sicut pretactum est)de presenti:aut distanti visu.

EN oultre/la diuersite des regars des choses obiectes/est tousiours a consi-
derer:mesmement de edifices. Car on les voit de front/ou par langle. Cest
adire par deuant/ou par le coing. τ les peut on veoir e quilateralmēt/ou inequila-
teralmēt:et de siege cōmun/ou esleue.et (comme il a este touchie dessus) x presen-
te/ou distante veue.

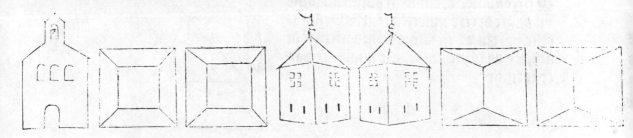

¶ In personis quoqz in eisdem statuendis/adequanda est quantitas
earum/ ad magnitudinem ipsozū edificiozum:vt singula rite quadzēt
et industriā artificialē redoleāt/ sicut per figuras videbiť.
¶ Et en statuāt ou asseant psonnes esd edifices/fault adequer τ conformer leur
quantite a la magnitude diceulx: affin que toutes choses aptemēt cōuiēnent/ et
redolēt ou representēt industrie artificiale cōme sera veu par les figures.

ADhuc notādum est φ res siue magnitudo visibilis (que est ma-
teria huius artis) quandoqz aspicitur vt ab ī-
tegro cōcipiať: τ tūc diameť piramidis seu triāguli
visualis/cadit ex directo sup ipam rē:vt constat p tetragonū hic positū:erectūquid τ eleuatū:quē qui to-
tū simul aspexerit argumētū ppositi tenebit.
ENcoz est a noter que chose ou magnitude visible(qui
est la matiere de cest art)est aucuneffoiz regardz pour
estre cōceue et cōpzise entieremēt: τ lozs le diametre de la pi-
ramide/ou triāgle visual/chet dzoitemēt sur icelle chose. Aisi
quil appt par le quadzangle cy mis/ erect τ est eue/iequel qui
tout ensemble regardera/largument du propos tiendza.

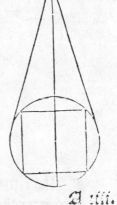

Nõnunq̃ aſpicitur / vt pars aliqua attentius intueatur / et tunc diameter piramidis ad ipſam partem quertitur / queadmodum acus horologii (qð quadrantem vocãt) ſi lapis magnes circumducatur: vt ſi quis ad cornu ſeu angulum dextrum inflexerit oculũ / illuc virtus viſiua transſeret piramidis diametrum / qð patet per figuram.

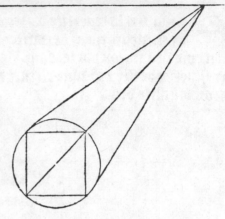

Aucuneſſoiz eſt regardee/affin q̃ aucune partie ſoit plus attẽtemẽt ĩtuite et parueue. et lors le diametre de la piramide eſt conuerti a icelle partie/ Ainſi que lecuille dũ horologe(dit quadrãt)ſe pierre daymãt eſt circonduit. Comme ſi aucun au corne ou angle dextre inflecte ɋ tourne lueil/a icelle part la vertu biſiue transportera le diametre de la piramide. Ce quappert par ceſte figure.

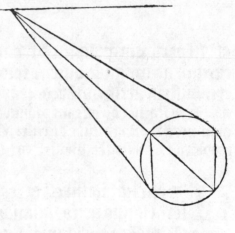

Qui vero ad leuum cornu reflexerit viſum:eius virtus ibidem reſeret ipſum diametrum vt figura pſens demonſtrat.

Et qui au corne ou angle ſeneſtre reflectera la beue/illec la vertu dicelle/reportera led diametre/cõme la figure pſente demonſtre.

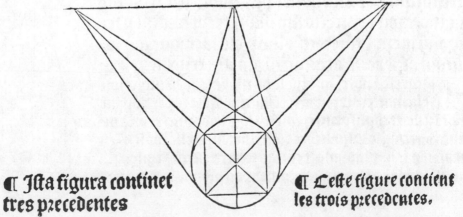

Iſta figura continet tres precedentes

Ceſte figure contient les trois precedentes.

Jnozatio autem tetragoni ſtrati coprehenditur per lineas viſu=
ales a pūcto ſubiecto ſuper inferiozes ſeu pzoximos eiuſd angu
los cadentes:et per ſectiōes diametroz piramidarū inclinatarū pzo=
tenſarum a terciis pūctis/duplo a ſubiecto remotis/vel amplius/aut
etiam minus/ſecundū ſedem fingentis: et pzeſentem aut diſtantē vi=
ſū. Circulus vero qui circa tetragonū erectū extat ſpheric⁹/circa ſtra
tum fit oualis/aut lēticularis/ſcōm differētias ſediū/et viſuū pzemiſ=
ſoz. Que pzopoſitiones/ſuper ſequentē figurā poſſunt coprehendi.

LA minozation du tetragone/ceſt adire du quadzangle/ſterne et couche/ou
giſant en plain/ſe compzēt par les lignes viſuales cheans ſur les angles
dicellut interiozes et pzochais:et par les ſectiōs des diametres des piramides in=
clinees/pzotendues des tiers poits/eſloignez du ſubiect/au double des pzecedens:
ou voiremēt plus/ou auſſi moins que leſ double/ſelon le ſiege du fingent/ et pze=
ſēte ou diſtāte veue: Et le ſercle qui entour le quadzāgle erect ſe dēmōſtre ſpheric/
eſt a lentour du ſterne et giſant/oual/ou lenticulaire: ſelon la differēce des ſieges
et veues pzemis. Leſquelles pzopoſitions ſur la figure ſubſequēte apperēt.

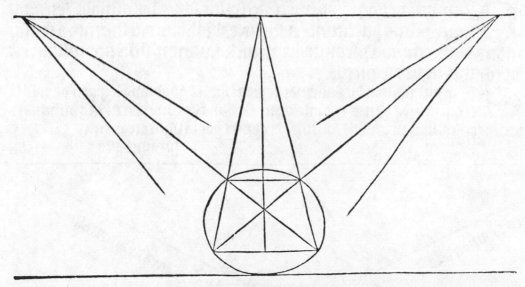

Alia deinde ſubſequens figura/tetragonum ipſum continet/abſqʒ
ſpherali circūferentia: remanentibus piramidibus pzemiſſis . Que
tamen piramides in ſingulis ſimilibus figuris nō ponenē in integrū:
ſed id ſolum ex eis quod erit neceſſarium. Licet ſuffingi/vel ſubintelli=
gi eas opozteat: vt conſtabit intuentibus.

A v

⁋ Lautre figure apꝛes mise contient le quadꝛangle sans circuference spherale: demoꝛãs les piramides pꝛemises: Lesquelles touteffoiz en toutes les autres sem∕blables figures ne seront pas entierement mises: mais ce seulement dicelles que sera necessaire. Combien quil les faille tousiours soubꝫfaindꝛe ou soubꝫenten∕dꝛe: cõme il apperra aceulx qui y regarderont.

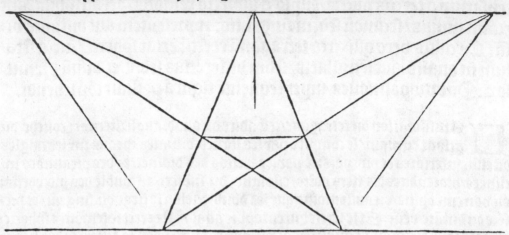

DIminutio quoqꝫ pauimẽti∕accipitur super huiusmodi tetrago∕num∕pũctis partitum∕ et lineis radialibus distinctum∕a sectio∕nibus diametroꝛum piramidarum inclinatarum∕sicut pꝛemissum est vt constat figura sequenti.

ET la diminution du pauemẽt∕se pꝛent sur les quadꝛangle∕parti de points et distinct de lignes radiales∕aux sections des diametres des piramides inclinees(cõme il est deuant touchie) et appert par la figure sequente.

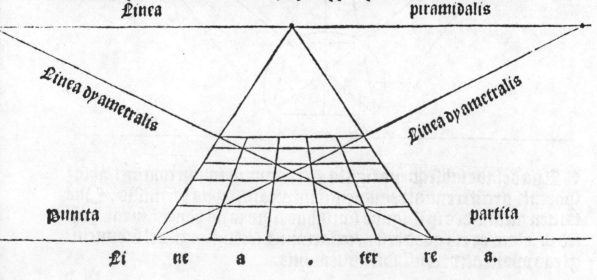

Linea   piramidalis

Linea dyametralis   Linea dyametralis

Puncta   partita

Li   ne   a   .   ter   re   a.

¶ Qi qui planiciei campestris spacia diminuere voluerit: protract
lineis rectis pauimenti sufficti/intentū habebit. Nisi alia geometrali
industria id facere pernouerit.

¶ Et qui veult limiter les distances despace chāpestre/en pourtraiāt les droites
lignes de pauemēt soubzfaint/aura son intencion: se par autre geometrale indu∫
strie naura cogneu le faire.

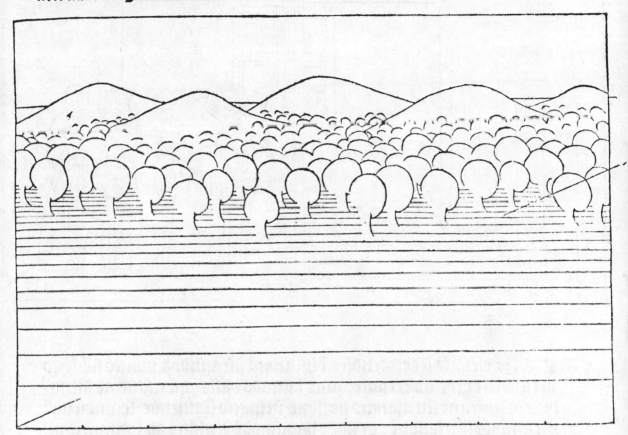

¶ Quantitas vero seu minoratio personarū:duobus modis accipitur
aut eni ex cōmuni:aut ex eleuata sede conspiciuntur. Si ex sede cōmu∫
ni:a/situ pedum earum capiuntur/& linea piramidali. Quam eciam
lineam/persone huiusmodi possunt a luminibus sursum excedere: vel
amplius in procerioze/aut gigantea magnitudine.

¶ Et quant ala quātite ou minoration des personnes (dont les plus esloignees
apperent a lueil/moindres que les prochaines) elle est prinse en deux manieres.
Car on les puet regarder de siege commun/ou de siege esleue. Se on les voit de

siege commun. on prent leur haulteur et minoration/de leurs piez/ a la ligne pi-
ramidale:laquelle ligne/ leſd perſonnes puēt exceder des yeux enſus:ou plus/ en
procere et giganteale magnitude.

¶ Si ex eleuata ſede:vtendū eſt inclinata piramide a puncto ſubiecto
vel altero ex terciis exeunte:cuius latitudo baſis/aperiatur ad altitudinem proxime ſeu maioris perſone in ſpacio ſtatuende: ſecundū cui⁹
piramidis iarctationē perſone huiuſmodi/ a plātis ad ſumma capi-
tum/ accipient minorationem:vt figura ſequenti:ordinata ſecundum
ſedem paulum eleuatam tantum/que tamē altius poteſt eleuari:etiā
ſupereleuari: et linea orizontalis/ac acies piramidis inclinate/ſimul
inaltari/prolongari ue/aut dilatari/vt prenotatū eſt/in articulo de figuris elementaribus:prout et plane comprehendetur ab intentis ſpe-
culatoribus.   Obicunqȝ autem pueri vel adoleſcētes erunt fingendi:
pro etatibus ſingulor veniēt in ȝtitate altitudinis metiendi:Quib⁹
pueris/ceteriſqȝ vbilibet aſſignatis pſonis/proportiones legitime da-
būtur pro magnitudinib⁹ ſuis.Et quod de pſonis per oīa dicitur:de ceteris animātibus ſimiliter intelligitur.

Se on les voit de siege esleue/fault vser de la piramide inclinee/y stant du point subget/ou de lun des tiers: de laquelle/la latitude basse/soit ouuerte a la haulteur de la prochaie et plusgrande personne quõ vouldra statuer en lespace. selon la in/arctation de laquelle piramide/lesõ psonnes prendront de la plante au hault des testes leur minoration. cõme appert par la figure ensuiuãte/ordonnee selon siege peu esleue/et se peut esleuer plushault/et encores suresleuer/et la ligne orizontale/et aussi la pointe de la piramide inclinee/ensemble esleuer/prolonger/ou dilater: ainsi quil est deuant note en larticle des figures elementaires; cõme auec ce sera cõprins des intes speculateurs. Et en qlque lieu que lon vouldra faidre enfans ou adol esces/sera leur quantite a prendre selon leurs aages: eu regart a la quan/tite des plusgrandes personnes: ausquelz enfans/et autres psonnes/ou que soiét assignees/pportions legitimes seront dõnees selon leurs magnitudes. Et ce q par tout est dit des psonnes/est entendu semblablemét des autres animaus.

Porro diminutio latitudinis colũnarum et similium rerum/acci/pitur ex diminutionibus tetragoni superelleuatis tanq̃ a basi/colũ nis et rebus huiusmodi. Altitudines vero cõstãt per piramides opor/tunas/iacétes scilicet aut pendentes/secundũ earumdem colũnarum sublimitaté/et vidétis sedem. Super quo et in visu nultũ distanti scu

lōginquo:expedit vti geometrali induſtria et ingenio. Similiterꝗ in
multis aliis/ſpeculationi argutioꝛ relictis.

℡ Et au regart de la diminution de la latitude et groſſeur de colūnes ꝗ ſemblables choſes/elle ſe pꝛent par la diminution du tetragone: eꝛ ſureſleuāt/cōme de la
baſſe/leſd colūnes ꝗ choſes. Et les haulteurs dicelles/ſe pꝛēnēt par piramides cō-
uenables/ Ceſtaſſauoir par les giſātes/ou pendētes:ſelon la ſublimite deſd colū-
nes/et le ſiege du voiant icelles. Surquoy/et en veue moult diſtante ꝗ eſloignee/
eſt expedient vſer ſouuēteſſoiz ꝙ geometrale induſtrie et engin:ꝗ ſemblablemēt/
en maintes autres choſes/laiſſees a la ſpeculation des plusargutz ꝗ ſubtilz.

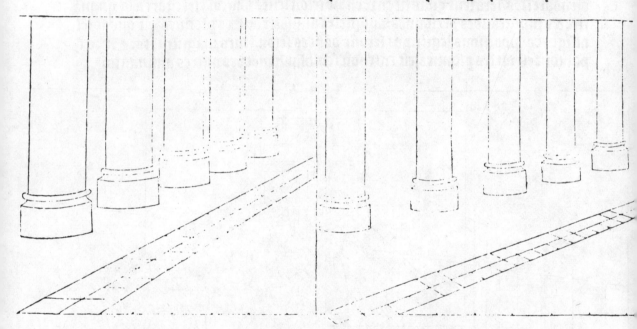

℡a x.

PRoinde (ſupꝛadictis ad effectū pꝛetenſū plane ſuſceptis) figure
exemplares ad inductiuā deſcripte videantur. Quarū nonnulle
ex memoꝛia ſtructurarū/ et picturarium quandoꝗ viſarum. Alie/ex
ipſa ſpeculatione ſunt erecte. Que concipiētur per elemēta pꝛemiſſa/
tanꝗ per litteras verba:Quipotius/ſuper huiuſmodi figuris intelli-
gentur eoꝛundē elementoꝛ officia:quoniam videlicet/planis foꝛmis
ſtatuendis (a quibus edificia huiuſmodi exurgūt) et rebus effingēdis/
ac cōmiſſuris/ſeu adunationibus earū/ maniductiuā habet aptitudinem. In figuris quidem edificioꝛ a fronte conſpectoꝛ/piramis recta
pauimentū cōſtituit:ꝗ due vel plures hincinde iacentes/lateꝛa ſeu pa-
rietes:Euerſa vero/teſtudinē aut tectum deſuper.

℡Onſequēment (Les choſes deſſuſdites/ a leffect pꝛetendu plainement
pꝛiſes) les figures exēplaires/ deſcriptes a inductiue/ſoiēt veues: deſqlles

aucunes sont erigees de la memoire de edifices ou paintures aucunesfoiz z piera veues: les autres/de la speculation du dictat. Lesquelles seront conceues par les elemes premis:côme sont parolles par les lettres. Ou mieulx/sur icelles figures seront entenduz les offices diceulx elemens: côme ilz ont aptitude manuductiue a statuer les plaines et plates formes/dont sont esleuez lesd edifices z'choses estingibles/ et a leurs assemblemens et adunations. Car es figures veues de plaine front/la piramide droite/ constitue le pauemêt:et deux ou pluseurs piramides gisantes côstituêt les costez ou paroiz:la euerse côstitue la volte ou toict dessus.

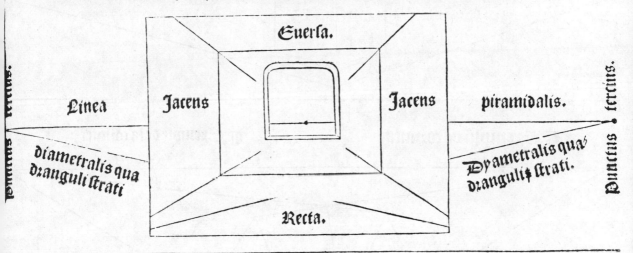

¶ In edificiis quoqz ab angulo conspectis duplex et diffusa ac bicornis operantur.

¶ Et es figures veues angulairemêt la double la diffuse z la cornue besoignêt.

¶ Exemplû de duplici.   **¶ Exemple de la double.**

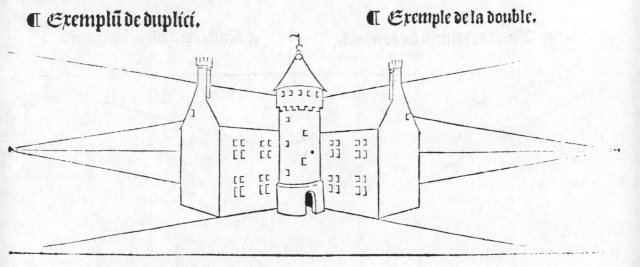

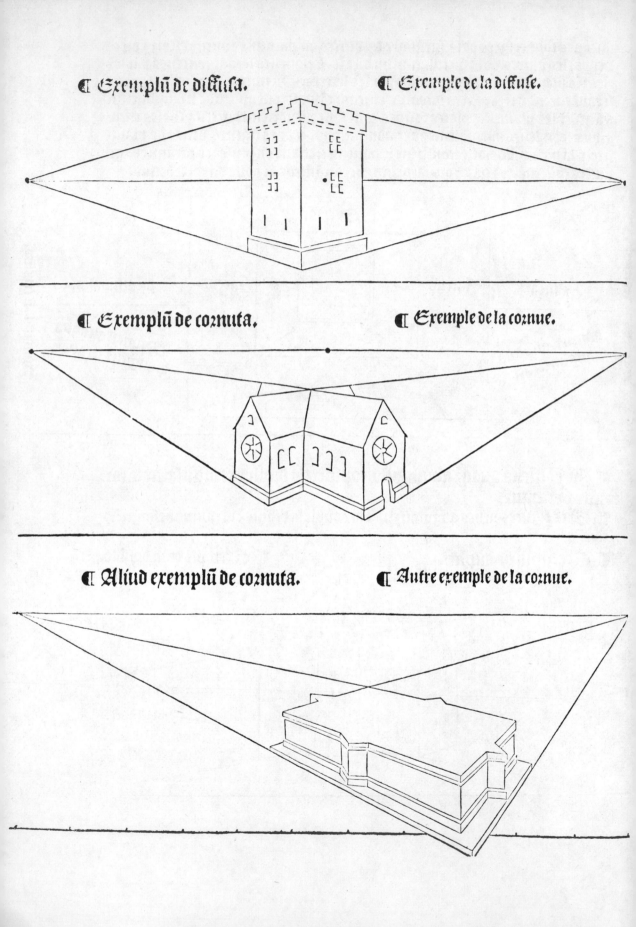

¶ Exemplũ de diffusa. ¶ Exemple de la diffuse.

¶ Exemplũ de cornuta. ¶ Exemple de la cornue.

¶ Aliud exemplũ de cornuta. ¶ Autre exemple de la cornue.

⁋ Pendens autē conuenit pluribus rebus:vt videbitur in practica.

⁋ Et la pendente/conuieat a pluseurs choses quon verra en practicant:

⁋ Aerea vero/nōnullis gradibus ponendis deseruit.

⁋ La aereale/sert a faindre aucuns degrez:

⁋ Cetera videbunt experimento ipsaru figuraru: Jn quibus tamē proportiones particulares personarum non obseruant precise:sed q̄; titates magnitudinū maxime:que/ ad propositū faciunt. Nec edificia protrahunt/aut variant ad omnē plenitudinē:propter spacior angu: stias/ et faciliorē conceptū artis et operis: Operisquidē non pictoris sed pictor et artificum/atq̄ omniū amatoris: Qui querentibus per: spectiue exordia qualia ex libris/ et designationibus ac oraculis peri: tissimor/ addita excercitatione/consequi potuit: fines leucor pertrā:

siens promere voluit. Præter que multa sunt/et artis/et nobilis pingendi subtilitatis archana: longa eruditione doctior/æ actuali rerum naturaliū atqȝ artificialiū cōtuitu/ et permensa obfiguratione exquirenda. Sculptor aute nodum tritor: ipsiusqȝ protrahētis sextā decadem transeuntis omissa/vel minus explorata/dirigāt videntes: leni peniculo perficientes omnia: Ad laudem summi artificis dei patris/ et filii: et spiritussancti. Qui ad perspiciendam regiam gloriosissime maiestatis sue/perducat omnes pacificos viatores terre: In qua/sicut patres nostri/aduene sumus/et Peregrini.

℅ Le sourplus sera veu par lexperiēce dicelles figures. Esquelles toutesfoiȝ les proportiōs particulieres des perionnes ne sont pas precisemēt obseruees: car cest vne autre maxime speculatiō/dont cy nest aucunemēt touchie: mais les quātitez de leurs grādeurs signāment/qui sont au propos: et les edificee ne sont pas pourtraiȝ ne variez ou enrichiȝ de fueillages et diuers signes/a toute plenitude/(car maītes choses se mettēt en grans volumes/qui sont demorees) pour les petiȝ espaces/et mesme de industrie ny ont este mis que les principaulx traiȝ/pour plus/facile cōception de lart et de leuure. Lequel euure nist de main de paitre mais de qui ayme les paitres et artisans/et touȝ biuās: qui aux querans les principes de la perspectiue dessus/quelȝ il a peu cōsuyȝ des liures/euures/æ oracles/ou collatiōs/de tresperiȝ/passāt par les fins de lorraine a voulu et este curieux mettre par escript. Oultre lesquelȝ principes/maits secretȝ sont de la noble subtilite æ paiture a querir par longue erudition de plusdoctȝ æ maistres en la science dite/et par actuel contuit ou regart/auec parmesurce obfiguration æ contrefacture des choses naturelles et artificiales. Ausourplus/les obmissiōs ou choses moins explorees des sculpteurs(non encores tritȝ ou frotez) et du pourtraiant passant la sirieme decade/vueillēt dresser les voiās: parfaisans le tout au pinceau doulx æ gracieux. A la louēge du souueraī artific dieu/pere/filz/et saīt espit. Qui a perspicer æ cōtēpler la cite roiale de sa souueraine maiestc/vueille produire touȝ pacificȝ viateurs de la terre: en laquelle cōme noȝ peres sōmes estraīgiers et Pelerins:

Pro cunctis orat fictor scriptorqȝ libelli
Cunctorū pariter supplicat ipse preces.

℅ Cellui qui a ce liure fait
Prie pour touȝ de cueur pfait
Et supplie treshumblement
Prier pour lui pareillement.

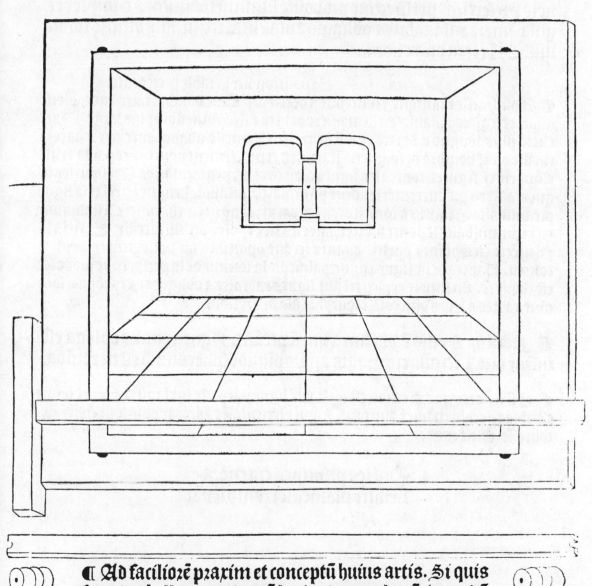

¶ Ad faciliozē praxim et conceptū huius artis. Si quis
fecerit tabellam quadzatā leuigatam ⁊ planā/in modū
effictē:latiozē tamen/sed et a dextris ⁊ sinistris longiozē
foliūq; desuper/cū cera tenaci aptauerit: omnes lineas
directas et perpendiculares/per tetragulā id est regulā
quadzū gerentē/ expedite pzotrahet. Quarū linearum
statuet pzimo duas principales/terreā videlicet ⁊ piza=
midalē: In quibus pūcta cuiq; congrua constituet: scili=
cet in piramidali/pūctum subiectū cum suis terciis/aut
altero eoz: Et in terrea/pūcta partita quotquot erunt
pauimento vel operi cōcepto opoztuna: Istis duabus li

neis præsertim / perspectiue propositæ summa cõducitur. Simplex regula / lineis radialibus ꝗ obliquis apta est: Circini / suis officiis conueniunt: Cetera discretioni.

Exposition sur la table precedente.

⸿ A plus facile praticque ꝗ conception de cest art / Qui vouldra faire vne tablette quarree legiere ꝗ plaine / en la maniere de la cy faite / touteffois plus large / Mais encor plus longue a dextre et a senestre: sur laquelle adapte auec cire tenace la fueille ou il vouldra besoigner: Il pourra expeditement pourtraire par la regle esquarre cy figuree / toutes les lignes droites et perpendiculaires. Desquelles lignes / asserra premieremēt les deux principales: assauoir la ligne terre / et la ligne piramidale: Esquelles constituera les pointz congruz a chacune: C'est assauoir en la piramidale / le point subiect / auec ses tiers poitz / ou lun diceulx: Et en la ligne terre / les points partiz / quants seront oportuns au pauement / ou euure conceu. Par ces deux lignes principalment / la somme de la perspectiue proposee est cõduyte. La simple regle / sert aux lignes radiales ꝗ obliques: Les cõpas / sont cõuenables a leurs offices: Le sourplus ala discretion.

⸿ Nota / ꝗ Sectio ē vbi linea lineã ptrãsit. figura oualis oblõga est / instar oui. Lēticularis magis appropiquat spherali: nõ est tñ rotũda.

⸿ Est a noter / que Section est quãt vne ligne parpasse sur lautre. figure ouale est oblõgue / ala maniere dun oeuf. figure lēticulaire approche plus de la spherale / touteffoiz nest ronde.

⸿ Qui les principes entendra
Leuure plainemēt comprendra

Sequntur figure exemplares / incipientes a varietate pauimentorum: quorũ quadratum / superius positũ / ca.ix° figura prima: principale est. Deinde figurãtur edificia / super plateas formas singulis aptas / et secundum ea que præmissa sunt erecta: vt patebit.

⸿ Cy apres ensuiuent les figures exemplares cõmencans ala variete des pauemens: desquelz le quarre deuãt nus / sur la premiere figure du ix° chapitre: est le principal. Apres sont figurez les edifices erigez et dressez sur les plates formes / cõuenables a chũn / et selon les choses dessus: cõme il apperra.

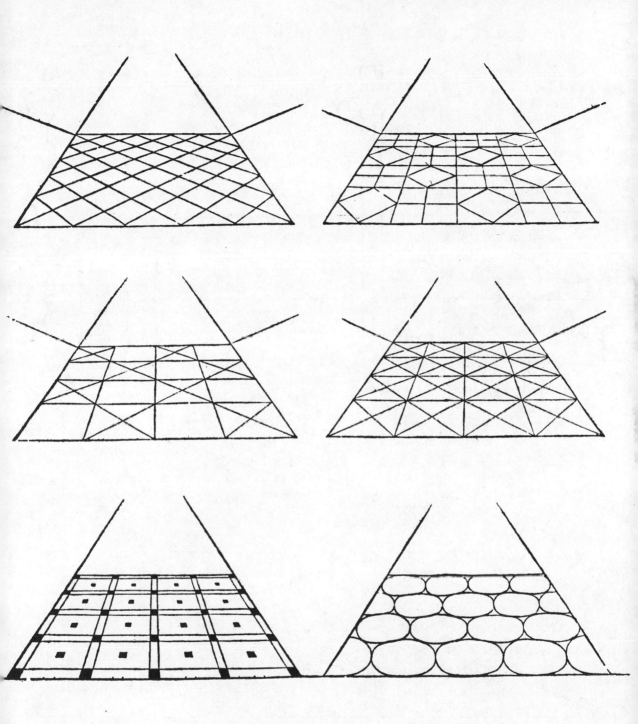

¶ Ainſi puet on et autrement /
Diuerſifier pauement.

B. i.

Signe / reboutant lennemi /
Garde du corps / de lame ami.

¶ Cest aux champs vne maison plate/
Ou il ne fault ne clou ne late.

B. ii.

¶ Telle maiſon que la preſente·
Et quatre cens liures de rente·

¶ Ci voit on la propre figure
Dune chambre et sa garniture

L. iii.

¶ Les ſōmiers / gouz / traueure / et tout:
Se rapporte de bout en bout.

¶ Aussi cler appert que lumiere/
La practique de la matiere.

℃ Excercice rend et eſtude
facilite et habitude.

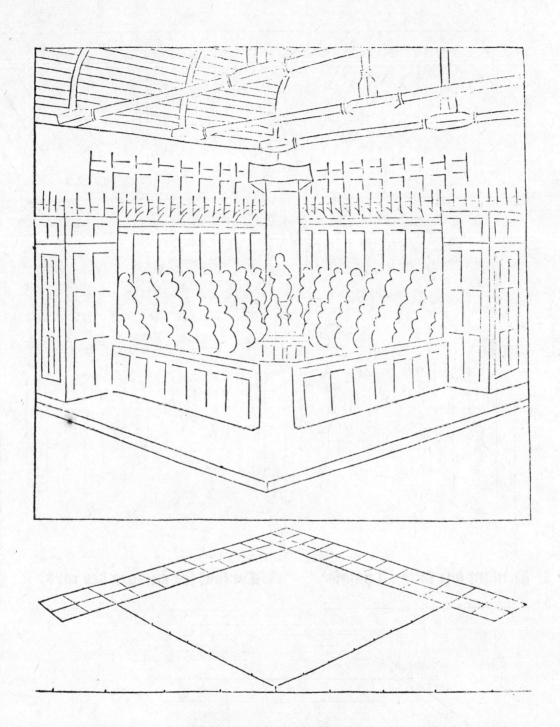

℀ faite fut / sur la souuenance
Du souuerain siege de france.

B. v.

ℂ Penſant aux ſales du palais⸳   Ou ſont les ymages des roys⸳

¶ Trente ans a / paſſay / en errāt
Du puy / ce pont / a mōtferrant.

¶ Telle forme ont (ainſi quon dit)
Les arches du pont ſaint eſpit.

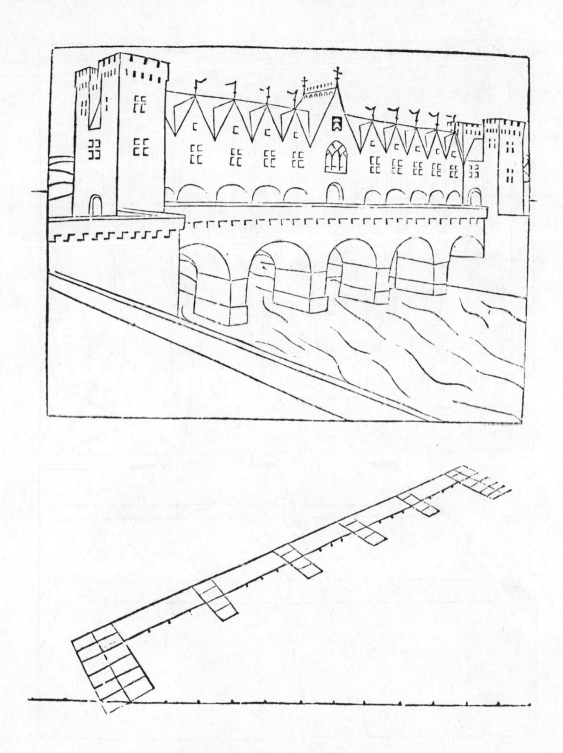

‖ Les arches / et tours / et maisons
Ont considerables raisons.

℃ Lignes / points / nombres / et figures /
Proportions / fault / et mesures.

¶ Les degrez / et la galerie.
Et tout fut fait par industrie.

C Restoir fault les chappemens
De propres varisiemens

¶ Toute bien faite pourtraiture/
Letifie humaine nature.

Chacune table tiēt par elle/ Chose differēte et nouuelle.

℄ Diuerſite de choſes ſert
A le faire trit et expert.

· T · IV · II · P · M ·

❡ Les colunnes et antiquailles
Sont magnifiques en murailles

L. i.

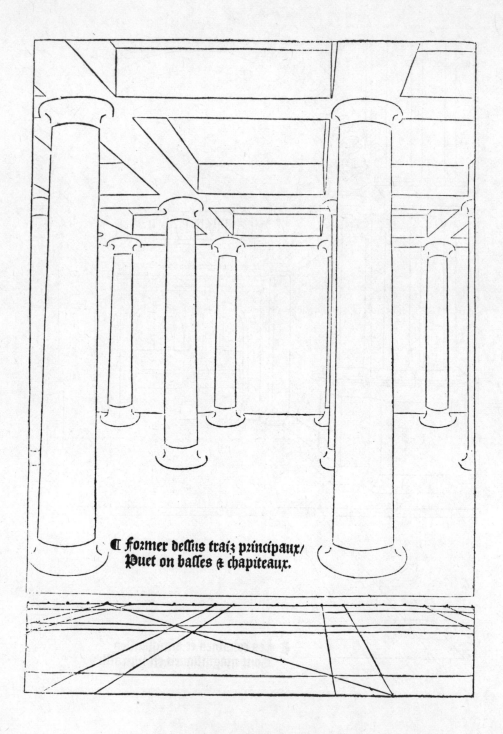

Former deſſus traiz principaux/
Puet on baſſes & chapiteaux.

¶ Recors des voltes et deuis
De nře dame de paris.

¶ Par art fait on habilement
Ce quest dificile autrement.

¶ Par tout ya collation
Dargute speculation.

L. iii

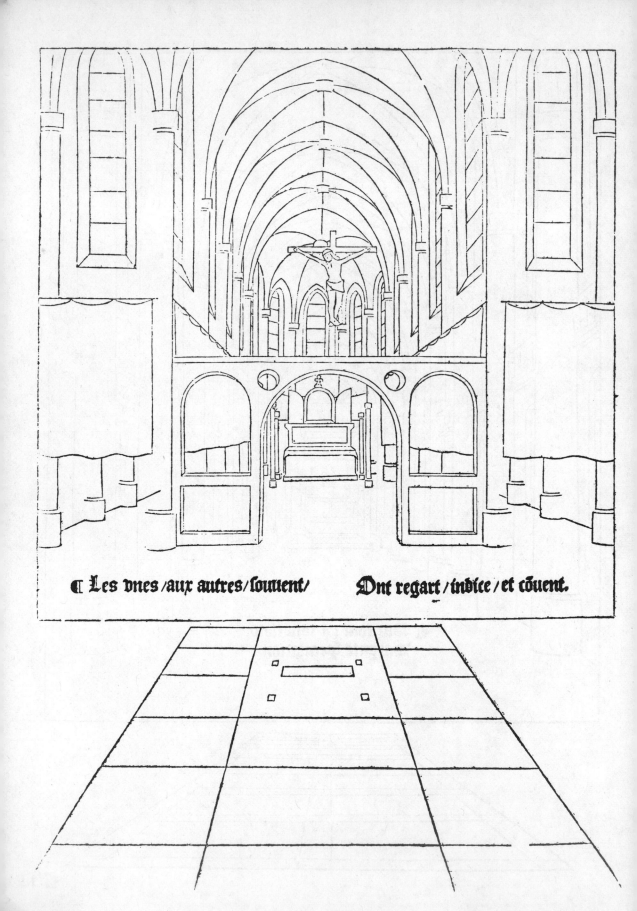

¶ Les vnes /aux autres /souuent/ Ont regart /indice /et côuent.

¶ Sur la memoire de leglise
Dangers / ceste forme fut prise.   C. iiii.

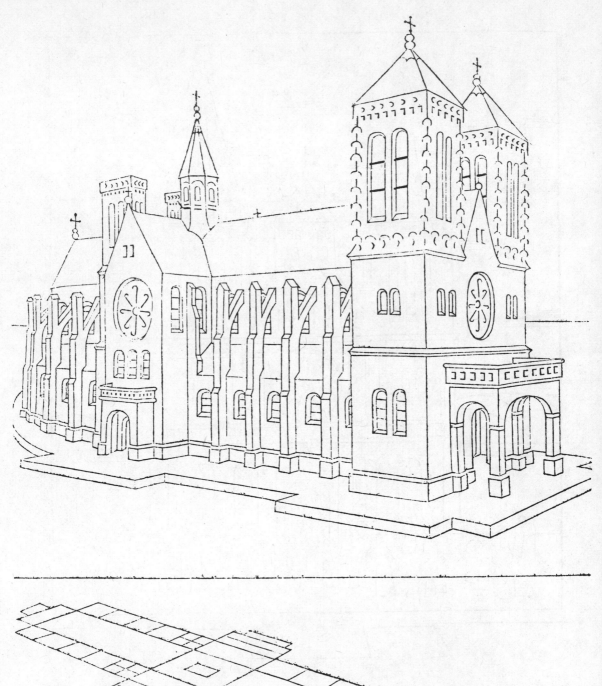

℃ La plate forme / lie / assemble /
Joint / et met tout louurage ensible.

℃ Qui vſent dart / et vſeront·
Diuuriers nõmez / ſont / et ſerõt.

ℂ. v.

Faire puet on / tours / & portaux /
Telz quil plaira / riches / & beaux.

¶ A choses faites / adiouster
Puet on / et changer / et oster.

¶ En la courcelle de louurier
De ce liure / a vng tel mourier.

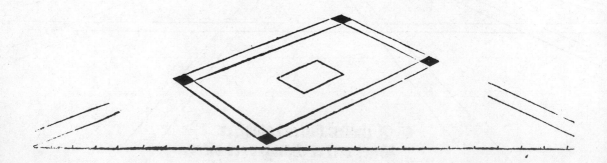

CARRETA·PELEGRINA*

⸿ En plain chemin / legierement·
En rude / allez tout bellement.

¶ Lombze fainte fur les quarreaux,
Juge le racours des touneaux.

℃ Les quantitez / et les diſtances /
Ont concozdables differences.

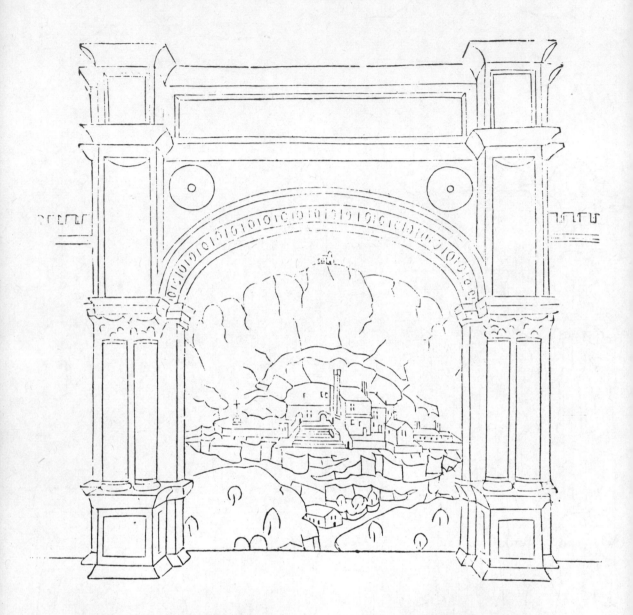

ℂ Par larc / au loing / la basme appt /	Exemple digne / et imitable /
Roche assise en reces desert /	Et lieu deuot / et visitable /
Haulte et rude: a vng antre obscur /	Pour se reduire / et enflamer
Lors ouuert / depuis clos de mur /	A la suyuir / et dieu amer :
Du iadis dure penitence /	Et qui ne puet faire la voye /
Fist la magdelaine / en prouence /	Son cueur par desir y enuoye /
Trente ans (dient) gisant sur terre /	En suppliant pareille grace /
Et plorant côme fist saint pierre /	Que dieu lui fist / Ainsi no⁹ face.

SVME · PATER · RERV̄ · QVI · PERSPICIS · OĪA · SOLVS ·
AD · TE · DIRECTO · CALLE · VIATOR · EAT · † AMEN ·

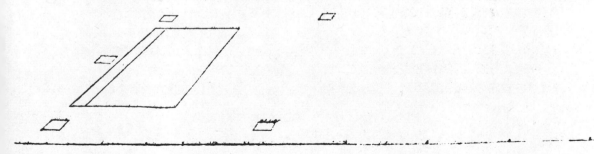

Impressum Tulli Anno Catholice veritatis
Quigētesimo nono ad Millesimū. iiii° Idus
Marcias. Solerti opera Petri iacobi pbr̃i Incole pagi
Sancti Nicolai.

✠ Sola fides sufficit.